PRAISE FOR *HUMILITY*

Bobb's book is countercultural in the best sense of the word, showing that even some of the singularly humble and charitable moments in our American political tradition—such as Lincoln's Second Inaugural—need to be enriched by the genuinely Augustinian insight from which our tradition has characteristically been deprived.

—PETER AUGUSTINE LAWLER, DANA PROFESSOR OF
GOVERNMENT, BERRY COLLEGE; EXECUTIVE EDITOR,
PERSPECTIVES ON POLITICAL SCIENCE; MEMBER,
PRESIDENT GEORGE W. BUSH'S COUNCIL ON BIOETHICS

Humility is essential to good character—and to our country. Only a humble nation—with humble leaders—will respect the people's natural rights. In this smart and lively book, David Bobb illustrates this virtue with the stories of five great Americans. And he reminds us that humility is at the core of our national creed of equality and liberty.

—PAUL RYAN

Nothing defies political correctness and the prevailing *zeitgeist* as radically as the notion that humility remains an important virtue. Dr. Bobb not only makes the case for this dismissed and disregarded value but emphasizes its importance as part of the American national character. This is a provocative and highly original book.

—MICHAEL MEDVED, SYNDICATED TALK RADIO HOST

David Bobb contends anew for the ancient theological virtue of humility and, indeed, for its definitive influence on the greatest Americans. A lively and counterintuitive argument, spiced with witty prose and engaging vignettes of Franklin, Washington, Madison, Lincoln, Frederick Douglass, and Abigail Adams.

—ROBERT FAULKNER, PROFESSOR OF POLITICAL SCIENCE,
BOSTON COLLEGE; AUTHOR, *THE CASE FOR GREATNESS*

In an age when expressions of national pride have become often brazen and increasingly wanton, David Bobb rightly seeks to remind us of the paramount virtue of humility. Setting before us several exemplary models of humble greatness, Bobb convincingly shows that the achievement of true greatness is not contradicted by humility, but perfected only through its cultivation.

—PATRICK DENEEN, PROFESSOR OF CONSTITUTIONAL
STUDIES, UNIVERSITY OF NOTRE DAME

Humility—and its correlative character trait, modesty—is the virtue most often forgotten today, when it is not actively suppressed or openly disdained by our culture. David Bobb has done us a wonderful service in writing a "biography" of the idea, providing a double example of humility in practice by drawing our attention to the essential humility of our greatest leaders and thinkers. Young readers will profit from this superb character instruction, while older readers can avail themselves of a mid-course correction!

—STEVEN F. HAYWARD, PROFESSOR OF CONSERVATIVE
THOUGHT AND POLICY, UNIVERSITY OF COLORADO,
BOULDER; AUTHOR, THE AGE OF REAGAN

Humility is a thoughtful and instructive study of American political and constitutional principles considered in the light of the Western political tradition. Organized around the most undervalued and overlooked of the virtues required for republican self-government, David Bobb's discerning study illuminates the pursuit of individual and collective political action from ancient to modern times.

—HERMAN BELZ, PROFESSOR OF HISTORY
EMERITUS, UNIVERSITY OF MARYLAND

With clarity and verve, David Bobb provides an instructive "biography" of the virtue of humility as it is manifest in the thought of the Western world and in American practice. His book ably demonstrates that humility is a precondition for healthy pride and true greatness of soul. His finely-crafted portraits of great Americans will be of interest to thoughtful citizens and seasoned students of American politics alike.

—DANIEL J. MAHONEY, AUGUSTINE CHAIR IN
DISTINGUISHED SCHOLARSHIP, ASSUMPTION COLLEGE

HUMILITY

HUMILITY

AN UNLIKELY BIOGRAPHY OF AMERICA'S GREATEST VIRTUE

DAVID J. BOBB

NELSON
BOOKS

An Imprint of Thomas Nelson

Published in Nashville, Tennessee, by Nelson Books, an imprint of Thomas Nelson. Nelson Books and Thomas Nelson are registered trademarks of HarperCollins Christian Publishing, Inc.

Thomas Nelson, Inc., titles may be purchased in bulk for educational, business, fund-raising, or sales promotional use. For information, please e-mail SpecialMarkets@ThomasNelson.com.

Unless otherwise noted, Scripture quotations are taken from the REVISED STANDARD VERSION of the Bible. © 1946, 1952, 1971, 1973 by the Division of Christian Education of the National Council of the Churches of Christ in the U.S.A. Used by permission.

Scripture quotations marked NIV are from HOLY BIBLE: NEW INTERNATIONAL VERSION®. © 1973, 1978, 1984 by International Bible Society. Used by permission of Zondervan Publishing House. All rights reserved.

Scripture quotations marked KJV are from the King James Version of the Bible.

Library of Congress Cataloging-in-Publication Data

Bobb, David J., 1974-
  Humility : an unlikely biography of America's greatest virtue / David J. Bobb.
    pages cm
  Includes bibliographical references.
  ISBN 978-1-59555-569-4
  1. Statesmen—United States—Biography. 2. Politicians—United States—Biography. 3. United States—Biography. 4. Humility—Case studies. 5. Humility—Political aspects—United States—History. 6. United States—Politics and government—1775-1783. 7. United States—Politics and government—1783-1865. 8. United States—Politics and government—1865-1900. I. Title.
  E176.B664 2013
  973.3092'2—dc23

2013022617

Printed in the United States of America

13 14 15 16 17 RRD 6 5 4 3 2

To Anna

CONTENTS

AUTHOR'S NOTE

Spelling, punctuation, and minor grammatical errors in the quotations from early Americans have been modernized. Misspelled names have been corrected, and abbreviations are spelled out.

PART I

EARLY LIFE

ONE

BENJAMIN FRANKLIN'S DILEMMA

Hundreds of years of expansion resulted in a vast territory in which its people lived in peace, united by a common tongue. Its military was the mightiest on the planet. No other nation could equal its wealth. It was the global leader in technology. Yet as the prosperity of the republic grew, the moral excellence of its elite faded. Adventures abroad brought the promise of greater glory but also the plague of war without end. Higher taxes on the wealthy failed to satisfy the growing appetite of a large bureaucracy. Transformed by a new set of leaders and transfixed by power, a once-proud republic became an arrogant empire.

For the revolutionary Founders of America, Rome's example was both familiar and unsettling. Having read Edward Gibbon's *The History of the Decline and Fall of the Roman Empire*, America's Founding Fathers sought to learn from his conclusions so that their new nation would avoid the imperial fate of Rome. "Immoderate greatness," Gibbon wrote, caused it to fall.[1] Early Americans knew that for their enterprise to become great, humility would be necessary. They also knew that of all the virtues of the human heart, humility is the most hard-won.

No one is naturally humble, but pride comes as easily to us as sleeping or smiling. My wife and I can see that almost every day in the lives of our two sons. In one unforgettable moment several years ago, our older boy reached an infant's peak of pride. Sitting upright without any assistance—flexing his flabby muscles of independence—our little explorer looked like he had summited Everest. An explosion of pride lit his face. Beaming, my wife and I reflected that pride back to our baby. "We're so proud of you!" we exclaimed.

It is a phrase a fortunate child will hear often enough to enlarge his heart but not so frequently as to swell his head. Just as pride comes naturally to human beings, so too does arrogance—or pride that exceeds the reality of one's merit. Arrogant people celebrate their own existence above all else and enlarge their own orbit at others' expense. To be proud of one's accomplishments, family, or country makes sense only if they are worthy of that pride. Healthy pride is tied to truth, and pride devoid of merit is arrogance. Humility's opposite is arrogance, not pride.

Though the virtue of humility is occasionally praised in some faraway tribe, remote religious order, or politician's rural birthplace, the reality of our fame-addled and power-hungry existence today means that arrogance is rewarded and humility is ignored. Ego trips are occasions for everyday media adulation. Cocksure, supercilious, and narcissistic displays of arrogance abound in every arena of life, while acts of humility go unnoticed and unheralded.

Our age of arrogance obscures the idea that humility is the indispensable virtue for the achievement of greatness. The personal significance of this idea is radical: to be truly great, one has to be humble. The political significance of this idea is profound: to be truly and enduringly great, a nation's hallmark must be humility. For Americans, this idea should have immense consequence, for our greatest moments have been marked by humility. Our future should be informed by that past. The lives of George Washington, James Madison, Abigail Adams, Abraham Lincoln, and Frederick Douglass have much to teach us about humility. Surprising as it may seem, "American humility" is not an oxymoron.

"IT'S HARD TO BE HUMBLE"

It's not easy at first glance to see how humility could ever lead to greatness. Humility hardly seems that good, let alone great. Implying something lacking—a loss of strength or a sapping of vitality—humility often strikes modern individuals as something to be avoided. Observed superficially, humility can appear weak and passive—anything but great. Greatness seems strong and energetic—anything but humble. "It's hard to be humble," Muhammad Ali is reported to have said, "when you're as great as I am."[2]

Humility *is* hard to achieve, even when you're not "the Greatest." It's more difficult to be great and humble at the same time. After all, humility requires exacting and often painful self-knowledge for any person but especially for one who thinks himself great. The humble person must acknowledge that he is not self-made, nor at the center of the universe. Unblinkered self-knowledge reveals our imperfections. Humility requires that we admit when we are wrong and then change course. It is the soul's state of self-knowledge in which we put others ahead of ourselves in thought, word, and deed—despite our tendency to self-aggrandizement.

The true power of humility is missed by many successful people today. *Why should I become a wimp?* the hard-charging individual wonders. Believing that humble folks must be shy and retiring, never forceful or magnetic, today's achievers cannot imagine themselves ever sitting on the sidelines. Humble people, they think, have poor self-esteem and probably even hate themselves. They're pushovers—meek, timid, and weak. To become humble in politics, business, or even in daily life is to give up on the possibility of impressive achievement.

In reality, humility is strength, not weakness. It is the crown of the virtues. Humility enables courage and points wisdom in the right direction. It is the backbone of temperance, and it makes love possible. Writing in the fifth century, Saint Augustine insisted that all people are capable of wearing this crown: "[T]his way is first humility, second humility, third humility . . . if humility does not precede and accompany and follow every good work we do," Augustine cautions, "and if it is not set before us to look upon, and beside us to lean upon, and behind us to fence us in, pride will wrest from our hand any good deed we do while we are in the very act of taking pleasure in it."[3]

Six centuries after Augustine, Saint Bernard of Clairvaux was asked to identify the four cardinal virtues. His purported answer: "Humility, humility, humility, and humility."[4]

"OVERBEARING, AND RATHER INSOLENT"

You don't have to be a saint in order to see the strength of humility. Long before he helped found a new nation, the twenty-seven-year-old Benjamin Franklin embarked on what he called "the bold and arduous project of arriving at moral perfection."[5] Impressed by the power of reason, Franklin decided that since he had knowledge of right and wrong, he could habituate himself always to do the right thing. Franklin's first step in his project was to list the virtues he would perfect. Temperance, silence, order, resolution, and frugality were the first five, followed by industry, sincerity, justice, moderation, and cleanliness. Tranquility and chastity made for a list of twelve, but a friend urged Franklin to add one more.

What Franklin's unnamed friend told him had to hurt a little, for as the Philadelphian wrote in his *Autobiography*, the man "kindly informed me that I was generally thought proud; that my pride showed itself frequently in conversation." Not content just to win an argument, Franklin sought to punish his interlocutors, his friend told him. Franklin was "overbearing, and rather insolent"— a prime example of unhealthy pride.[6] The solution for Franklin quickly became obvious: he would add humility as the thirteenth virtue he would tackle. Humility's dictate according to Franklin was simple to state, if not easy to do: "Imitate Jesus and Socrates."[7]

Franklin formulated a careful plan of attack for all thirteen virtues. Take the first, temperance, remember its basic idea ("Eat not to dullness; drink not to elevation"), and work on it with special vigilance for a week.[8] Acts of intemperance would earn a "little black spot" in Franklin's little book of virtues.[9] An unspotted page on temperance would indicate mastery. Each week would bring another virtue into focus, even as Franklin continued to work on the virtues from preceding weeks. With thirteen virtues, the virtue-a-week program allowed for four full cycles each year. Annual repetition of this "self-examination," he hoped, would make him into a self-governing individual.

Despite the pleasure he took from his project, Franklin admitted that humility proved the most elusive virtue of all: "I cannot boast of much success in acquiring the *reality* of this virtue; but I had a good deal with regard to the *appearance* of it."[10] In this, at least, he was partly successful, for as Franklin moderated his tone in argumentation, he started not just winning arguments but also winning people over to his causes. This humility in rhetoric worked wonders, Franklin found. Looking back over the course of his life, Franklin claimed that his efforts at becoming more humble were rewarded. Whether in making proposals for "new institutions, or alterations in the old," Franklin attributed his success to his continued exertions. Calling himself a "bad speaker, never eloquent," even prone to stumbling, Franklin discovered that his fifty years of effort at humility produced a considerable power of persuasion.[11]

Though he made progress in checking his pride, Franklin found that its temptation endured. Healthy pride can become harmful arrogance if a person is unguarded against it. At the same time, this temptation grew for the new nation. "In reality," Franklin wrote in 1784, "there is, perhaps, no one of our natural passions so hard to subdue as *pride*. Disguise it, struggle with it, beat it down, stifle it, mortify it as much as one pleases, it is still alive, and will every now and then peep out and show itself." This conclusion made sense to Franklin because he had wrestled with pride so much in his own life. "[Y]ou will see [pride], perhaps, often in this history," he wrote in his autobiography, at the age of seventy-eight, "for, even if I could conceive that I had completely overcome it, I should probably be proud of my humility."[12]

Franklin's dilemma is America's dilemma. Pride is a national, as well as a personal, challenge. Though Franklin's autobiography was written before the United States had a great deal about which to be proud, that struggle would intensify as America ascended to new heights of power and wealth. Learning how to become humble—and stay humble—was a perennial challenge. Like the young Franklin, young America possessed an extraordinary ambition for significance. Both aspired to be great. How can a nation be humble and stay humble while at the same time achieving greatness?

Whether ancient or modern, political rule is more often associated with an exertion of arrogance than a demonstration of humility. When we speak of politicians and humility, it is often to refer to the "roots" of one who rises up from poverty. When a politician talks of humility, it is often after a stinging defeat or a stunning victory. Invariably, no matter the outcome, a politician is proud of his campaign. And inevitably, in our current climate, political opponents cast each other as the archetype of arrogance. The old saying that a statesman is a dead politician might be updated: a statesman is a politician with humility.

"THE EXCELLENCE OF HUMILITY"

The five humble heroes featured in this book—Washington, Madison, Adams, Lincoln, and Douglass—are proof that greatness and humility need not be opposed to each other. All five individuals were great in soul and humble at the same time. The thirteenth-century theologian Saint Thomas Aquinas argued that humility and the high virtue of magnanimity, or greatness of soul, are twins. Magnanimity guides the gaze of great individuals to the heights. Humility issues a warning against flying too high. As Thomas stated about humility, it "represses rather than adopts a pushful and self-confident temper."[13]

Pushful. That word captures much about human striving. "Pushful" people seek greater power and recognition at the expense of others. They are puffed up with their own worth. The men and women of American history profiled here were not immune to "pushfulness" or puffery. They were not born humble any more than they were born great. Humility came no easier to them than it did to Franklin. The trials and temptations they faced were unrelenting.

Had George Washington let pride get the best of him, the world might remember him as the man who betrayed the Revolution by crowning himself king. James Madison was tagged as weak and timid, but the humility he learned as a brilliant legislator helped him mold the new nation. Without the humility that made her so resilient, Abigail Adams might have despaired at the plight of women as a whole. Instead, Adams made the best of her abilities and her situation and helped rear a young republic.

If Abraham Lincoln had not humbled himself, he might have become a dictator. In preserving the Union and ending slavery, Lincoln lived up to the humility of the American Founders and gave the generations that followed—black and white—a worthy sense of pride in their nation. If Frederick Douglass had abandoned the humility he acquired in the midst of humiliations, he might have become embittered and unforgiving. If pride had gotten the better of him, he might have lost all goodwill for his fellow citizens. Instead, keeping pride in check, he upheld hope—for himself, his family, those previously ensnared by slavery, and all Americans. Humility helped him reach many who otherwise might not have listened to the message of equality and liberty for all.

Before we explore these examples of extraordinary humility, however, we need to examine the nature of the virtue itself. The next two chapters will provide a condensed history of humility, starting with Socrates and Aristotle in ancient Greece, then moving to the words and example of Christ, then to Augustine and the fall of Rome in the fifth century after Christ, and still later to Aquinas, Machiavelli, and Thomas Hobbes.

After the fall of Rome, Augustine wrote the *City of God* "to convince the proud of the power and excellence of humility, an excellence which makes it soar above all the summits of this world, which sway in their temporal instability, overtopping them all with an eminence not arrogated by human pride, but granted by divine grace."[14] Humility offers the promise of excellence, but it does not guarantee power when power is the proud domination of human beings. The power promised by humility is power over oneself in self-government. It is much harder to achieve. Humility's strength is hidden, obscured by our blindness and the age of arrogance in which we live.

JESUS AND SOCRATES

enjamin Franklin set out to "imitate Jesus and Socrates" in his quest to be more humble. In describing his dilemma—and America's—Franklin did not tell his readers exactly what his *imitatio* entailed. Did the lives of Jesus and Socrates teach him the same lesson regarding humility? Or did they represent different aspects of this vital virtue? Could a person be humble and have a great soul at the same time? Franklin says much in his *Autobiography* about his process of self-improvement, but he does not delineate the precise role the examples of Socrates and Jesus played in his plan.

The history of humility is a crooked line, for the classical and Christian ideas of the virtue are at odds with each other. For many leading Greek and Roman thinkers, humility was not even a virtue in the way Christianity later conceived it. According to Aristotle— whose teacher, Plato, was a student of Socrates—the great-souled or magnanimous man answers to no one but himself. He seeks virtue and is awarded the highest honor for his greatness. But according to Augustine, writing some 750 years after Aristotle, the idea of a great-souled man acting independently of God was the height of arrogance. A humble prince, Augustine insisted, must bow before God and other citizens who are not as worthy as he is of honor. Like Aristotle's mag-nanimous man, the humble prince seeks virtue, but his virtue, unlike that of the magnanimous man, is marked by compassion, mercy, and prayer—not pride in his own accomplishments or honors accorded by others. Augustine's ideal prince is a servant.

Niccolò Machiavelli, writing a millennium after Augustine, concluded that both Aristotle and Augustine were wrong. The ancient pagans held a pie-in-the-sky view of politics where virtue was the goal and honor was the reward. This view, Machiavelli held, neglected the fact that most human beings are not morally upright; they are moved by power, not virtue. Ancient Christians were no more realistic: their kingdom was not even of this world! How could Christianity expect to make princes capable of keeping power or citizens capable of wanting powerful princes? Machiavelli's leader is willing to embrace a certain kind of pride and yet pretend to be humble if it serves his interest. Arrogance would be folly, not because it is morally wrong, but because it is ineffective. For Machiavelli, execut-ing good rule meant the death of heartfelt humility.

"YE SHALL BE AS GODS"

According to the Genesis account of creation, God created the first human beings good—even perfect. They "fell" away from that state of perfection when, succumbing to temptation, they sought to be like God. "Ye shall be as gods," the serpent told Eve, able to know good and evil (Gen. 3:5 KJV).

"The beginning of pride is sin" (Sirach 10:13). This was one of Augustine's favorite biblical verses. In his hands it helped to shape the Christian doctrine of what came to be known as "original sin." Articulating this doctrine is simple, as schoolchildren in early America learned from their primers: "In Adam's fall we sinned all."[1] Explaining it, however, is a different matter. When Adam and Eve fell from grace, the doctrine teaches, no person born after them would be capable of complete goodness. Furthermore, as Augustine explained, "The effect of that sin was to subject human nature to all the process of decay which we see and feel, and consequently to death also."[2]

For Augustine, the arrogance of Adam and Eve, seen in their eagerness to defy God and seek to be like him, had a tragic parallel in the angelic fall that preceded theirs. It was an "arrogant angel," Augustine argued, that led the human beings down the same path: "With the proud disdain of a tyrant he chose to rejoice over his subjects rather than to be a subject himself; and so he fell from the spiritual paradise." Arrogance twisted the angel into existence as a serpent who was forced to live in regret. He "was to worm his way, by seductive craftiness" into convincing human beings to join him in his fallen state.[3]

Augustine's view of humility and pride in human beings was linked to his view of love. While expounding the idea of original sin, Augustine also upheld the existence of unconditional divine love and high achievement by human beings. He described pride as a misbegotten intimacy or love: instead of responding to God's love and drawing closer to him, the first human beings retreated into the recesses of their hearts. In so doing they became less themselves— less like God created them to be. They departed from their nature, which was perfect until they turned from God. Unhealthy pride pushes man away from God; it destroys his ability to cling to his Creator as he should, not in miserable self-debasement, but in worshipful humility. "Now it is good 'to lift up your heart,'" Augustine urged, "and to exalt your thoughts, yet not in the self-worship of pride, but in the worship of God. This is a sign of obedience, and obedience can only belong to the humble."[4]

The garden of Eden left Christianity one of its fundamental ideas: excess pride is self-worship that shrivels the soul. Pride promises that the self will be exalted, but the promised exaltation turns out to be false. Humility alone offers the possibility of real exaltation. Augustine explained this paradoxical notion: "But devout humility makes the mind subject to what is superior. Nothing is superior to God; and that is why humility exalts the mind by making it subject to God."[5] Refusing one's place in the eternal order is a supreme vice. The Old Testament God punished the disobediently prideful human beings who insisted on exalting themselves. Pride goes before the fall.

"NO WORSE MAN THAN YOU ARE"

Not every ancient civilization deplored pride and celebrated humility. Many, in fact, saw pride as a virtue and humility as a vice, or at least unworthy of praise. Thought to be derived from the word *humus,* or earth, the word *humility* conjured for many in the ancient world the idea of baseness.[6] Lowliness—or literally, being close to the ground—was not an accomplishment worthy of praise. On the contrary, the lower one is to the ground, the more loathsome one is. Why would a great man stoop to be lower, to bring himself closer to the dirt? Rulers required their subjects to bow low before them—perhaps even to touch the ground—in a gesture that established for all to see the hierarchy fixed between the great and the lowly. For most ancient Greek and Roman thinkers, a humble existence was by definition an abject existence. It was unthinkable that a man might be exalted by being humble. Greatness and humility were separated by an unbridgeable chasm.

To understand this world, which is far removed from our own egalitarianism in its emphasis upon a stratified social order, we might best turn to the depiction in Homer's *Iliad* of the lowly yet loquacious Thersites. Known to history only from a few short passages, Thersites nonetheless makes an unmistakable impression upon any reader of the epic poem. "This was the ugliest man who came beneath Ilion," Homer said of Thersites, referring to Troy, in what is now Turkey. "He was bandy-legged and went lame of one foot, with shoulders stooped and drawn together over his chest, and above this his skull went up to a point with the wool grown sparsely upon it."[7] Known for upbraiding his superiors, Thersites delighted the throngs of soldiers who would assemble to hear his harangues.

Upon one such occasion, Thersites confronted King Agamemnon, the commander of the Greek forces, for his dogged pursuit of a decade-long worthless war against the Trojans. Waged to reclaim Helen, a woman lost by the Greeks, or Achaians, to the Trojans, the war had stretched on without resolution for ten years, leaving troops on both sides exhausted and ill-tempered. Thersites challenged Agamemnon, saying, "Son of Atreus, what thing further do you want, or find fault with now? . . . It is not right for you, their leader, to lead in sorrow the sons of the Achaians. . . . Let us go back home in our ships." After this stinging rebuke, the golden-tongued Odysseus, king of the Greek island of Ithaca, rushed in to halt the brazenness of Thersites. "Stop, nor stand up alone against princes. Out of all those who came beneath Ilion with Atreides I assert there is no worse man than you are. Therefore you shall not lift up your mouth to argue with princes, cast reproaches into their teeth, nor sustain the homegoing." With those words, the "brilliant" Odysseus, "sacker of cities," whacked Thersites with his kingly scepter. Thersites, stunned, "sat down again, frightened, in pain, and looking helplessly about wiped off the tear-drops" from his face.[8]

Like the serpent in the garden of Eden, Thersites was condemned to crawl—if not quite on his belly, then at least on his knees. Whereas the ancient Christian tradition said that God would humble the proud, the ancient Greek tradition dictated that the proud would humble the insolent. Odysseus was proud—a prince who ruled by right of nature—and so were all the other Achaian rulers. No one so low as Thersites could challenge their supremacy. The gap between ancient traditions is clear: humility, an exalted virtue for the ancient Christians, was for the ancient Greeks sheer folly.

Odysseus's expectation was not that Thersites would be humble; rather, it was that he would know his low place and stay there, for-ever. There is an important difference between these two concepts. Odysseus used his scepter as a weapon of subordination; his action had legitimacy because of his social and political standing. There was no way for Thersites to speak truth to power, for however repugnant the manner of his speeches was, the underlying problem was that he dared to speak out against the rulers at all. (That Homer gives Thersites words that ring true might tell us something about Homer's sense of justice.) For the ancient Greeks, one's high or low station determined how one should act. If an individual was of high and noble birth, to lower oneself by acting lesser than one's station was shameful. If one was of low birth, to strive for anything beyond one's natural allotment was wrongheaded. To have pretense to a higher station was to act contrary to nature. Pride, then, was a virtue reserved only for the high and well-born. The low were lowly for a reason, and crowning their inferior place in life with the consolation prize of humility served no purpose.

Although happy to celebrate the virtue of pride, the ancient Greeks had a limit on what level of pride was acceptable or healthy. Hubris, their idea of disordered pride, marked an unsavory overconfidence. Hubris blinds the person whose head it has swollen. In the *Iliad*, it was Achilles who was blinded first by rage and then later, hubris. "Sing, goddess, the anger of Peleus' son Achilles and its devastation, which put pains thousandfold upon the Achaians," Homer began his poem.[9] Having slain Hector, Troy's crown prince and best warrior, Achilles dragged the dead man's body behind his chariot for nine days and otherwise defiled the body. This act of hubris was halted only when the Trojan ruler, King Priam, begging on his knees, prevailed upon Achilles to stop abusing the body of his son so he could bury him. In the end, Nemesis, the goddess representative of what is due, had her revenge. Paris, son of Priam, brother of

Hector, and cause of the whole conflict as the one who ran away with Helen, shot an arrow that found its way to the heel of Achilles, killing him. For the ancient Greeks, hubris went before Nemesis.

"WHAT ONE DOES NOT KNOW"

Even though Socrates cited Homer more than he cited any other poet, the Athenian philosopher helped to bring about a moral and political order worlds away from that depicted by the blind bard. Replacing raw courage with unyielding reason as the crown of the virtues, the philosophical revolution of Socrates gave rise to a new hierarchy of virtues in which arrogance and pretense were deplored. So how did Socrates end his life on trial for what amounted to a kind of hubris? Was he, in fact, as Benjamin Franklin held, a model of humility?

Even in the golden age of Athens, five centuries before Christ, people did not subject their thinking to the rigorous scrutiny of philosophical inquiry more than any other era. It was his life's mission as a "gadfly," Socrates said, to sting people into such thinking.[10] An inner voice, what Socrates called his *daimonion*, would not allow him any other pursuit but the truth, no matter where that journey led. Not exactly conscience, and not revelation from on high, Socrates's *daimonion*, the political scientist Thomas West has suggested, was more like an inner prompt that arose out of his very nature. We should not think of it as an external "voice," but rather more like his essence—that without which he would cease to be the same man.[11] Socrates engaged others in dialectical conversations ranging over many topics including piety, courage, justice, and friendship. Like Jesus, Socrates never wrote anything, but as the Platonic dialogues demonstrate, Socrates was a master at destroying the assumptions held by his interlocutors. He claimed not to be a teacher, but there were plenty of people who said they were his students.

What did he teach? And for what did he stand? These questions were front and center at the classical world's trial of the millennium, held in Athens in 399 BC. Socrates's answers at the trial to these questions was recounted by Plato. A friend of Socrates, he claimed, went to the Delphic oracle and asked whether any man was wiser than Socrates. No one was wiser, the oracle responded. Incredulous at this claim, Socrates immediately sought to prove the oracle wrong by attempting to discover a wiser man than he. Searching among the politicians, poets, and craftsmen, Socrates found not wisdom but only its pretense, especially when it came to "the greatest things." Real wisdom is never pretending "to seem to know what one does not know."[12]

Many people throughout the ages, including Benjamin Franklin, have discerned a striking humility in this insight and in Socrates himself. Not many people of Socrates's own day drew the same conclusion. They saw arrogance instead of humility—a heart beating to self-exaltation, not the sublime. They felt that his humility was false, that behind his humble mien lurked a subversive spirit bent upon corrupting the young by denigrating the city's faith. An indictment of three charges was thus brought against the seventy-year-old Socrates: he had refused to acknowledge the gods of the city, he had introduced new divinities, and he had corrupted the youth. In addition to these formal charges, there was also an older rap against Socrates—that he inquired into what we would call astronomical questions and that he was a sophist who taught the young to be careless about the truth.

The trial of Socrates was held just five years after the oligarchy of the Thirty Tyrants in Athens had ended. The memory of the trouble wrought by the young autocrats lingered freshly in the minds of the approximately five hundred jurors, most of whom were old men. It did not help Socrates's cause that two of the Thirty, including its leader, Critias, were formerly part of his circle. Another such interlocutor was the traitor Alcibiades, responsible for immeasurable grief on both sides of the Peloponnesian War waged between Athens and Sparta from 431 to 404 BC. For his part, Socrates did not defend himself against the appearance of guilt by association. Instead, he relied upon his contention that he had never been a teacher.

The defense Socrates mounted against the charges was astonishingly anemic. He himself was surprised that the narrow guilty verdict against him was not more decisive. When the trial moved to the penalty phase, Socrates's rhetoric turned from feeble to fantastic. Given the Athenian legal tradition that permitted a proposed counterpenalty by the defendant, Socrates advanced the idea that instead of death he should be given free meals for life in the Prytaneum, which was reserved for heroes of sport and war, public benefactors, and the descendants of the greatest Athenians. If this had happened in America, it would be like Socrates proposing that he take up permanent residence in the White House's Lincoln Bedroom.

The *megalegoria*, or "big talk," of Socrates at his trial struck his accusers, and the jurors, as the height of hubris. It got him the hemlock. And it may leave some asking, how can he possibly be considered by Franklin or anyone else a paragon of humility? The humility of Socrates is found neither in his personal behavior nor in his rhetorical excesses. It is found, rather, in his obedience to duty. Socrates subjected himself to reason. He felt responsible not mainly for his family, his city, or even his own life, but rather to the constant call of reason. His single-minded allegiance impelled him on a courageous journey whose peak was philosophy. Reflecting on politics and the just regime, or form of government, became a supremely important task; for without the protection afforded by a well-ordered regime, philosophy was subject to the same tyranny of opinion that handed Socrates his death sentence.

"THE HONOR OR THE FEAT IS A GREAT ONE"

In Plato's account of Socrates, we see a depiction of the man of thought. In Aristotle, Plato's student, we find a depiction of the man of action. Aristotle's brush strokes are at their most vivid in his portrait of the magnanimous man in the *Nicomachean Ethics*. According to Aristotle, the peak of the virtues is pride, properly understood. This virtue he called *megalopsychia*, literally "great-souledness" or "magnanimity." To be magnanimous is not, as we think today, to be generous (that was the virtue of liberality or, if done on a grand scale, magnificence). Rather, to be magnanimous is to have the right estimation of one's worth when one's worth is great. This virtue is extremely rare. It is not accessible to all, for not everyone lives at the high level of achievement in war or politics required of the magnanimous man. (And for Aristotle, the virtue of magnanimity was reserved to men, as war and politics were their domain.) This is the stuff of statesmen of the highest order, not city managers.

Aristotle, who counted among his young students Alexander the Great, knew something about the study of power, politics, and ambition. As critical as questions of power and ambition were for political leadership, even more important was the question of which virtues were most important for citizenship. Each virtue, for Aristotle, marked a mean between two extremes. Courage, for example, is the mean between the vicious extremes of cowardice and rashness. Magnanimity is a mean between the extremes of vanity (taking too high a view of oneself) and pusillanimity (taking too low a view of oneself). As the proper estimation of one's worth when one's worth is great, magnanimity is not accessible to many.

"The Few. The Proud. The Marines." Magnanimity is not in the tagline, but the idea of the marines is about the closest thing today that captures the idea of great-souledness. Standing not only for the absolute commitment to excellence in everything they do, marines also perform their duties for the right reasons. Honor, their most sacred possession, is the result of their virtue.

For Aristotle and his fellow ancients, pride, properly under-stood, presupposed the unalterable fact that certain individuals are more virtuous than others by nature. Some souls are philosophically inclined; others, including those who march to the drumbeat of war, are men of action. For Plato, some men are natural-born guardians of the city, or political regime. All men were not created equal. Not in their rights, not in reflecting some image of God or the gods, and not really in any other way. Plato and Aristotle concurred: men are marked more by inequality than anything else. "Be all that you can be" was the U.S. Army's slogan for just over twenty years. Of this slogan Aristotle might wonder, *But what if all you can be is good, not great?* Not everyone can be great. That was Aristotle's bottom line.

Like the marines, the magnanimous man lives by honor. It is that by which he judges his virtue, the pursuit of which is supreme for him. Magnanimity, Aristotle says, is the crown of the virtues, "because it enhances them and is never found apart from them." True magnanimity "is impossible without all-round excellence."[13] The magnanimous man is proud of his extraordinary virtue and worthy of only the most important honors. Even then, his greatness is ultimately defined by virtue, not honors. While arrogance distorts an individual's view of himself, magnanimity is evidence of perfect clarity of vision. This is not to suggest that the magnanimous man is perfect—only that his understanding of himself must be true.

In the fourth book of the *Nicomachean Ethics*, Aristotle wrote what might be considered a mirror for the magnanimous man. One entry in the classical genre of mirrors for princes, Aristotle's contribution was for an especially exclusive audience. Not for princes of just any sort, it described those whose aspirations were of the highest order. Usually chock-full of advice, the mirror genre was a cross between a political playbook and a self-help handbook. Some mirrors gave leaders a chance to see themselves as they were. More commonly, mirrors gave would-be leaders a chance to see themselves as they could become.

According to Aristotle's mirror, the magnanimous man avoids both "petty risks" and unnecessary dangers, "because there are few things that he values highly."[14] The magnanimous man would excel on the battlefield, but if the battle was not great enough, he would almost certainly not consider fighting. Aristotle's description of the magnanimous man calls to mind a great statesman rising to meet and defeat a challenge posed by an invidious foe—Winston Churchill, for instance. According to Churchill biographer Carl Bechhofer Roberts, the confident leader knew all about Aristotle even before he read him. Having been given a copy of the *Nicomachean Ethics* by a friend, Churchill returned it to him, writing approvingly, "But it is extraordinary how much of it I had already thought out for myself."[15]

For Aristotle, pride was not bad or evil. If maintained in the proper amount, it was a worthy thing. In Aristotle's mirror, the magnanimous man is almost godlike in his independence. He does not rely upon others for assistance, much preferring to make others his debtors and beneficiaries. He is "eager to help others."[16] He is haughty toward those perceived to be influential, but he moderates his pride in dealing with inferiors (no need to lord his superiority over lesser people). Eschewing contests, the magnanimous man "hangs back or does nothing at all, except where the honor or the feat is a great one."[17] You would not find a magnanimous man on a reality television show. He rarely expresses admiration, for little or nothing about other people is great to him. Forgetting wrongs, the magnanimous man does not engage in personal conversation, not wishing to hear compliments of himself or criticism of others. Unless he intends to insult someone, he is generally not given to abuse. Reluctant to request help, he prefers beautiful but unprofitable possessions "because this is more consistent with self-sufficiency."[18] With a wink of his eye, Aristotle notes of the magnanimous man that it is often said of him "that his gait is measured, his voice deep, and his speech unhurried," all further indications of his imperturbability.[19]

The magnanimous man has no need for anyone else, but he is happy to have a friend. The problem is that friendship implies equality, and there are precious few who are equal to the truly magnanimous. This fact makes the idea of honoring a magnanimous man difficult, for to receive honors from inferiors is not especially honorable. When no one is your equal, much less above you, who can honor you? The magnanimous man would not show up for the Attican Chamber of Commerce awards dinner.

The supreme self-reliance of the magnanimous man implies the lack of two other traits: humility and piety. He does not admit any deficiency. He is not dependent upon external goods, and he seeks, by dint of his own accomplishments, independence from the vicissitudes of fortune. Even though he values certain honors, he pays little heed to those who would honor him. Humility for the magnanimous man would require him to deny his own magnanimity, for it would make him see others as his equals.

Some three centuries after Aristotle, a teacher in Palestine preached a message that would scandalize anyone who might have thought himself magnanimous.

"HE WHO HUMBLES HIMSELF WILL BE EXALTED"

No social, religious, or even political hierarchies were immune from Jesus' message of equality before God. All human beings are in need of salvation, he proclaimed. Each is equally sinful. This introduction of spiritual equality brought with it the inversion of political and social hierarchies. Real sovereignty rested not with earthly powers but rather on high. The King of kings ruled a kingdom not of this world, and humility was his crown. Kingdoms of arrogance everywhere, beware!

Just as pretentious and powerful citizens of Athens were stung by Socrates's questions, so too did the Sadducees and Pharisees, religious leaders of Jesus' day, frequently feel the sting of his rebukes. They did not even have good intentions in Jesus' characterization of their hypocritical and thus false humility. Throughout the Gospels, especially the account given by Luke, humility is a virtue enjoined by Jesus in both word and deed. The Sadducees and Pharisees were blind to their own vanity.

For Jesus, unlike Aristotle, the only sure remedy was external to oneself. "I am the way, and the truth, and the life," Jesus Christ said, claiming to be not only the way to God but God himself (John 14:6). Jesus' claim was taken by many in his day as the ultimate presumption, the epitome of arrogance. To his disciples and followers, Jesus' actions demonstrated nothing of the cockiness with which he was charged. He had come as an infant, after all, and was born in a manger. He had nothing of the highbrow or haughty in his actions. Instead of hobnobbing with the rich and powerful, Jesus hung out with the poor and lowly. He extolled the virtues of those considered outcasts, praising qualities usually associated with society's undesirables. He even washed the feet of those thought untouchable. In lowering himself to the ground, to touch the lowermost parts of the lowliest people, Jesus demonstrated that he did not hold himself higher than them.

"Blessed are the meek, for they shall inherit the earth," Jesus said in his Sermon on the Mount, preached near the end of his earthly existence (Matt. 5:5). However much "the meek" might conjure up an image of cowardly pushovers, the truth is far from that perception. People with the gift of meekness do not inflict injustice. Meekness is the strong denial of the power of oppression. Jesus showered love upon those least expecting it—the poor, the downtrodden, the physically infirm, the socially outcast, and the politically unpopular people of his day. His ministry to them came at the expense of time spent with the wealthy, influential, and beautiful people. His example was outrageous in his day, for it flew against all of the rigid hierarchies of power and privilege that marked Roman rule. His actions scandalized even the religious leaders, who largely had been swept up by the same superciliousness toward "lessers" that characterized the actions of the political leadership. Even those Jesus ministered to were startled by his being with them, so accustomed to being ostracized had they become. In loving the misfits of his community, Jesus outraged those who had been blinded by excess pride. "Truly, I say to you," Jesus taught about the judgment to come, "as you did it to one of the least of these my brethren, you did it to me" (Matt. 25:40).

Just as Jesus extolled those who were meek and humble, so too did he excoriate the arrogant. In parables especially, Jesus assailed those who are consumed by their pride. In one such story, Jesus told of a Pharisee who, having seen a tax collector praying nearby, offered his own public prayer: "God, I thank thee that I am not like other men, extortioners, unjust, adulterers, or even like this tax collector." The pleas of the tax collector, unlike those of the Pharisee, were sincere: "God, be merciful to me a sinner!" he begged. Jesus' response was unmistakably clear, as he said of the tax collector, "I tell you, this man went down to his house justified rather than the other; for every one who exalts himself will be humbled, but he who humbles himself will be exalted" (Luke 18:9–14). Not a promise of earthly rewards or a grant of political power, the exaltation pledged by Jesus lifts the human soul to spiritual liberty.

In other parables and sermons preached by Jesus, children figured prominently. With small stature, spiritual openness, and inquisitiveness of the soul, children personify humility and the honesty it demands. For Jesus, none were greater. He rebuked those who would "hinder" the children from coming to him (Matt. 19:14). "Truly, I say to you," Jesus proclaimed, "whoever does not receive the kingdom of God like a child shall not enter it" (Luke 18:17). A worthy disciple of his, Jesus said, should emulate a child, "for he who is least among you all is the one who is great" (Luke 9:48).

Even as Socrates had toppled the ideological hierarchy of his day, elevating reason and philosophy above all else, so also did Jesus upend the order of virtues and vices of his day. Rejecting assertiveness in pursuit of worldly success, and success pursued at any price, Jesus redefined not just the ends of a good life but also the means by which people should achieve them. Out were the goals of domination, lordship, and self-promotion. In were the ends of service and self-denial. Sharp elbows and words of wrath had to go. "Pushful" people have no promise of prosperity. Kindness, patience, and purity defined the means by which people should strive to be servants. "The Son of man came not to be served but to serve, and to give his life as a ransom for many," the gospel of Matthew says of Christ (Matt. 20:28). Still, all of this meekness did not mean weakness. Jesus was not outfitting a merry band of wimps. He did not come to equip an army either. His message was that the struggle was spiritual and the reward eternal. Earthly treasures were nothing when compared to the spiritual riches one could store in heaven. All the striving on earth is for nothing if not directed to God. This message he delivered with unwavering resolve, sometimes with a little child in his lap and other times with a scourge in his hand. No milquetoast messiah, his word was that love would lift the lowly to the loftiest place and that those who saw themselves as high and mighty would be brought to their knees in submission before the almighty God.

"Greater love has no one than this, that he lay down his life for his friends," Jesus said (John 15:13 NIV). Putting his own words into action, Jesus was crucified on a cross, or what Augustine called "the wood of humility."[20] Just as some mistook Socrates for a sophist, or one who sold pseudowisdom for profit, so too did some of Jesus' contemporaries suspect him to be a Zealot, bent upon ushering in God's kingdom on earth. While a minority saw his work as zealotry, many more saw Jesus as a prophet, pursuing a mission clearly recognizable as such from historical antecedents.

Despite his clear statements that his kingdom was not of this world (John 8:23), Jesus was suspected of having political motivations. This suspicion is understandable, for many thought his stated intentions of apolitical ministry would be abandoned as soon as his popularity would allow. And even if the Roman rulers believed his stated political reserve, Jesus' teachings on otherworldly rule brought an even more powerful and long-lasting threat. Instead of fearing that their subjects would follow a usurper, rulers feared that their subjects would proclaim loyalty to a completely different principality. This shift would entail not just throwing out one ruler for another, but rather a full-fledged regime change, for a Christian's ultimate loyalty is to an invisible kingdom. The Romans quickly realized the seismic shift about to occur. Humility before God, for Christians, might mean the increasing irrelevancy of political powers. The insistence that a particular regime could command absolute loyalty would fade. No political ruler would be able to command submissiveness. Jesus did not come to preach a political message, but his gospel had earthshaking political consequences.

THREE

THE CITY OF THE HUMBLE AND THE CITY OF THE PROUD

I t took awhile for the aftershocks of Jesus' political-religious earthquake to be measured. And it took Augustine, one of the early church fathers, to try to explain the tremors. He did so prompted in no small part by the sacking of Rome by the Visigoths in AD 410, which according to many prominent people of his day was caused by Christianity. Such critics charged that the Christian attitude to politics, with its loyalty to a kingdom to come, depleted Rome's strength and resiliency, leaving it vulnerable to the invaders. At the same time, Christianity offered no coherent political system of its own and sapped Roman *virtù*, or "fighting strength," of its vitality. Augustine counterattacked with vigor. The accusers of Christianity should look instead at their own vices, he said, for the pride Romans took in their political and military edifice ensured not strength but weakness. It was only a matter of time, Augustine argued, before the entire structure would collapse. No external cause, especially Christianity, was to blame.

Born in AD 354 in North Africa, in what is now Algeria, Aurelius Augustinus was no stranger to prideful living. Raised a Christian by his mother, Monica (who later became a saint), Augustine rebelled against the faith of his youth and found his talents in wordsmithing. With an electric mind for language, Augustine became what he later described as "a salesman of words in the markets of rhetoric."[1] From the ages of nineteen to twenty-eight, he was caught up professionally in the pursuit of what he later called "the empty glory of popularity." As he admitted in his *Confessions*, "Publicly, I was a teacher of the arts which they call liberal; privately I professed a false religion—in the former role arrogant, in the latter superstitious, in everything vain."[2] In his personal life he was morally lax. At the age of thirty, Augustine was appointed the city of Milan's official orator, in which role he delivered a panegyric, or official praise poem, for the Roman emperor Valentinian II. Augustine later concluded that his rise in the world of the Roman elite was marked by "the spirit of the school of pride."[3]

Two years after he had delivered a paean to the emperor, a moral and intellectual awakening in Augustine freed him from his arrogant ways. "Return to you," he cried out to God, "is along the path of devout humility."[4] The first step for Augustine was being brought low in submission to the divine. "Proud people may laugh at me," he wrote. "As yet they have not themselves been prostrated and brought low for their soul's health by you, my God."[5] Augustine's rebirth as a Christian saw him rise as rapidly in the church as he had in the secular world; just eight years after his baptism, Augustine was appointed bishop of Hippo, in North Africa. As he balanced his many duties as pastor, preacher, counselor, bishop, and even judge, Augustine discovered that his political role was inescapable.

The sacking of Rome prompted Augustine to reconsider the prevailing idea of citizenship. The results of his thinking shaped not just the Christian idea of citizenship but the secular as well, for Augustine proposed the idea of "two cities" that define the ultimate allegiance of human beings. The City of God and the City of Man are built on opposing loves. A citizen of the City of God loves God; a subject of the City of Man loves himself first and in this selfishness loses himself in pride. The City of God is the city of the humble. The City of Man is the city of the proud. In the City of God, divine love is the shared goodness that increases rather than decreases with additional sharers. In the City of Man at its worst, it is confusion—not goodness—that is shared in common. Within the City of Man, the best that can be hoped for is that a concern for property, a limited material good, can be shared.

Augustine explained the gap that separates the cities with reference to two sets of twins, who taken together were the founders of the City of Man: Cain and Abel, the sons of Adam and Eve; and Romulus and Remus, the founders of Rome. Cain's murder of Abel marked the founding of the earthly city. The quarrel between Cain and Abel reveals the relationship of the City of Man and the City of God. The story of Romulus and Remus reveals what transpired after human beings fell from grace and embraced evil, for in doing so they plunged themselves into a constant struggle for glory. The founding of Rome, the most visible exemplar of the City of

Man, reflected that acrimony of Cain and Abel. Disordered pride prompted the bloodshed in both cases, for Cain and Romulus both committed fratricide with envy born of arrogance. Romulus's desire to be the only founder, an arrogant assertion, motivated him to kill his brother, Remus. Romulus did not want to share glory or power. This is the fundamental law of the City of Man: politics, like life, is a zero-sum game. The more one's fellow citizens have of power or resources, the less there is available for others. The political state as exemplified in the Roman founding, birthed because of the original sin of pride, is beset by pride. Pride begets more pride until its weight is unbearable. Augustine cited Rome as the prime example of this unfortunate truth: "And the lust for power . . . first established its victory in a few powerful individuals, and then crushed the rest of an exhausted country beneath the yoke of slavery."[6]

The *libido dominandi*, or "lust for power," is the political equivalent of original sin, the most obvious manifestation of pride in politics. It, like pride as the original sin, is so powerfully corrosive that no merely human effort can prevent its corrupting effects. Just as original sin degrades the original perfection of human nature, so too does the *libido dominandi* weaken the claim to justice in politics. The political realm attracts individuals who love power, so the danger of pride is always present in political rule. The ruler, puffed up with pride, readily believes himself to be autonomous, his own lawgiver.

In Augustine's analysis, if the ruler forgets that he is not God, in effect he crowns himself god. Yet to the pagan ruler—and the defenders of the old pagan Roman order that Augustine engaged—it would seem only natural that a ruler, especially an emperor, should love glory above all other things. In the Roman world, the pursuit of power and honor is the very definition of nobility, so to deprive a ruler of his glorification is to remove from politics its highest goal.

"THEY ARE BUT MEN"

To help Christian rulers guard against the temptation of pride, Augustine presents his own "mirror" in book five of the *City of God*. Augustine's mirror for Christian princes presents a reordering of the hierarchy of the virtues usually suggested for sound political rule. In it he elevates humility to the highest place rather than political cleverness, effectiveness, and strength. For Augustine, Christian rulers were blessed, or happy, not because they had "long reigns," were able to bequeath their thrones to their sons, "subdue" their enemies, or quell insurrections at home. They are blessed with spiritual and ultimately eternal reward if they stay true to the compassionate and merciful ways commanded by God. The usual rules for leadership that were typical of power politics did not apply.[7]

Glory must not be sought for its own sake. The temptation of pride must be actively combated. These are the presuppositions that guided Augustine in the making of his "mirror," which consists of twelve characteristics befitting the blessed Christian ruler. Starting with the necessity of just rule, Augustine emphasizes that the good prince must resist the "voices of exalted praise and the reverent salutations of excessive humility" or else be inflated with pride. In an age in which Roman emperors routinely claimed they were divine, Augustine reminded them "that they are but men." As mortals, they must respect and serve their Creator and help those under their rule to do the same. They should do so with mercy and compassion, always aware that "more than their earthly kingdom, they love that realm where they do not fear to share the kingship."[8]

Augustine knew that many of the Roman ruling class to which he was directing his advice saw political rule as a means to gain honor and power. He also knew that the classical definition of a tyrant was a ruler who used his office to aggrandize himself at the expense of the common good. Do not use the office for personal vengeance, Augustine counseled. Good rulers will hold in check "self-indulgent appetites all the more because they are more free to gratify them." They should "prefer to have command over their lower desires than over any number of subject peoples." Intentions matter, as all of these things should be done "not for a burning desire for empty glory, but for the love of eternal blessedness." To keep straight, Christian rulers must offer God "as a sacrifice for their sins, the oblation of humility, compassion, and prayer."[9]

Augustine's mirror is a bold statement because it informs Christians that neither the emperor nor the state can ever be the means of salvation. No one, including Christians, should try to make politics the means by which souls are saved. Because arrogance deadens the conscience, it must be guarded against not only with real humility but also the practice of true compassion. Pride's temptation must be repelled because if arrogance wins out, the result will be tyranny that overtakes the soul.

Aristotle's magnanimous man and Augustine's Christian prince both are said by their authors to do great things. Their motivations are very different, as are the means by which they are to achieve great things. Although Augustine did not offer a direct critique of Aristotle because Aristotle's writings were unavailable to him, Augustine's critique of Rome could apply equally well to the magnanimous man. In his view, both the Romans and Aristotle's magnanimous man lacked the piety that would keep pride in check. If the magnanimous man would reply to such criticisms (he would not be so inclined, given his nature), he would say that he is entitled to his feeling of pride. It would be dishonorable and disreputable for him to feel inferior about his great accomplishments.

To Augustine, this position is still arrogant. No matter how great one's accomplishments appear to oneself—or to the world—they are nothing compared to the greatness of God. The magnanimous man sits precariously atop his peak. His self-reliance, ostensibly his strength, is actually his weakness. With self-reliance comes the constant danger that virtue, supported by nothing but willpower, will collapse into vice. Just as the vaunted Roman quest for glory easily degenerated into the lust for domination, so too might the magnanimous man's love of his own virtue and the resulting honors lead him to a life of domination. And even if it did not lead to such a terrible end, where in his life is real love, service, or self-sacrifice? From the Christian view, such a life lacks all these things. The magnanimous man cannot wear his crown of virtues unless he puts on humility.

For the philosopher Karl Löwith, "The Christian virtues are not natural and reasonable virtues of a golden mean but radical virtues of grace."[10] In Christian teaching, human beings are dependent upon God. That is the heart of Jesus' message about humility. We also are meant to be with others, to depend upon others, and to care for others. True humility enables true compassion. It helps us know that we should care for others, especially for those who have less than we do. That ethic is largely absent from Aristotle and the ancient world. Take the way in which Aristotle described those who have accomplished less than the magnanimous man: "The man who is worthy of little consideration and thinks that he is such is temperate, but not magnanimous, because magnanimity implies greatness, just as beauty implies a well-developed body: i.e. small people can be neat and well-proportioned, but not beautiful."[11] The magnanimous man will not advance himself at the expense of those who are weak, but neither will he go out of his way to help them. A magnanimous man will not kneel to wash anyone else's feet.

"A PRAISEWORTHY ABASEMENT"

Writing some eight hundred years after Augustine and drawing significantly upon the African church father as well as Aristotle, Thomas Aquinas argued that humility and magnanimity are complementary, not opposing, virtues. Taken together as twins, they help human beings accomplish things of excellence. In making magnanimity a virtue, the Christian thinker Aquinas had to remove the magnanimous man from his high horse. Whereas Aristotle's magnanimous man is not pious, Thomas's is. Having acquired a sense of deference before God, the magnanimous man assumes a new and improved identity in Thomas's depiction. Where it is difficult to picture Aristotle's great man engaged in full-time ministry to the poor, Aquinas's touched-up version shows a magnanimous man who is more attentive to the needs of others.

Aquinas made humility and magnanimity twins in part because the magnanimous man meets his Maker. That amendment to Aristotle is notable. Understood as Aristotle and Augustine advanced their respective ideas of magnanimity and humility, the two virtues are incompatible. Thomas's repositioning of Aristotle's idea of magnanimity reveals an important possibility for our inquiry, for in modifying the idea of magnanimity he makes their compatibility more likely. Wresting magnanimity away from Aristotle's definition allows us to see the virtue in new light. In separating the magnanimous man from submission to the divine and to others beneath him, Aristotle cuts him off from humility. Overconfident in his self-completeness, the magnanimous man's crown of virtue in reality is incomplete. It is for that reason that Aristotle's magnanimous man seems somehow defective—harsh, devoid of love, and aloof from the things that ennoble our humanity. To be humble and great-souled—wholly given to excellence in virtue for the highest causes, and yet eager to serve God and others in all things—is to accomplish something even rarer and more impressive than the virtue depicted by Aristotle.

Humility, Thomas wrote, is "a praiseworthy abasement."[12] It is not self-debasement. "Consequently," he explained, "the role of humility is not to repress our appetite for high and difficult projects, but rather to keep a sense of proportion in our reckoning."[13] If true humility keeps aspirations in line by reminding man of his limits, healthy pride helps propel him to greatness by reminding him of his possibilities. Politically, healthy pride also helps man understand his sense of place in this world. It tells him to stand up for himself, his family, and his country, and to keep striving to make himself and those to whom he belongs better. He becomes great in soul when he becomes wholly given over to the pursuit of virtue, desirous of honor for the right reason and determined never to forsake his virtue. He is great in soul when humility resides in his heart, and he becomes selfless in his love for others. Greatness of soul is reserved to the few not because few are called by nature but because few are able to achieve the mastery of pride it requires.

"TO LEARN TO BE ABLE NOT TO BE GOOD"

In 1513, more than a thousand years after Augustine wrote his mirror for princes, Niccolò Machiavelli wrote what has become the most famous, and infamous, mirror. Titling his book of advice *The Prince*, Machiavelli dedicated it to the "magnificent Lorenzo de' Medici," the ruler of Florence. Machiavelli promised that in his slim volume he would "go directly to the effectual truth of the thing" rather "than the imagination of it."[14] Taking a swipe at Socrates, Plato, Aristotle, and the entire classical tradition on the one hand and Augustine and the Christian tradition on the other, Machiavelli declared his frustration with those who were unrealistic in their political expectations. The imagined republics conjured up by the ancient pagans were delusional. For classical and medieval Christians, it was "the kingdom to come" talk that did not add up. Either way, politics was subjected to moral imperatives that ultimately did not make sense. "[B]ecause [men] are wicked and do not observe faith with you," Machiavelli announced, "you also do not have to observe it with them."[15] This inversion of the golden rule defines Machiavelli's new politics.

"Men are not good." In this conclusion Machiavelli found common ground with both the ancient pagan and the Christian traditions, neither of which viewed man as fundamentally good or perfectible. But where ancient philosophers and Christian thinkers sought to raise human beings up from their low starting point, Machiavelli's teaching would allow them to linger there—if that was necessary to accomplish the end of maintaining power. An aspiring prince knows the value of being good, what he needs more is "to learn to be able not to be good."[16] What is most important is not the achievement of good, but the appearance of it. A prince "should appear all mercy, all faith, all honesty, all humanity, and all religion."[17]

A prince can also pretend to be humble. But he should never lose the pride that is fueled by his ambition. The end, or goal, is power—gaining it, retaining it, and passing it on. The "new modes" and "new orders" that Machiavelli urged for the prince meant that he should not fear using vice as well as virtue in the pursuit of power.[18] Imitating Aristotle by including eleven virtues in his catalog just like the ancient thinker had in his *Nicomachean Ethics*, Machiavelli placed not magnanimity but moral flexibility as the crown. Don't worry about the means to the end, Machiavelli counseled the prince. And don't think of virtues as ends in themselves or blessings beyond our earthly existence. If effective, just do it. If ineffective, let your enemies blunder into it. Stick to what hits the target, even if that means keeping a quiver of vices ready at hand.

Aristotle urged individuals to pursue greatness if they were one of the few capable of greatness. Augustine countered by claiming that the only way to be great is to be good. Feign goodness, Machiavelli said, if it will allow you to achieve greatness. Aristotle or Augustine? Socrates or Jesus? Machiavelli's solution would make

Benjamin Franklin's dilemma vanish, along with any worry about moral perfection or which virtue ought to be the crown. Get real, he said, and find leaders who are not hung up on old, irrelevant ideas; we need a new and improved mode of leadership.

"THE MORTAL GOD"

The Englishman Thomas Hobbes, like Machiavelli, was a realist about human beings. He harbored no illusions about their goodness or perfectibility. In fact, Hobbes believed that their imperfections were the distinguishing mark of equality. Like Machiavelli, Hobbes also worried that the elevation of certain virtues would in fact diminish the political order. More than any other political thinker, even Machiavelli, Hobbes dedicated his life's work to fighting the twin threats to politics posed by humility and magnanimity.

Hobbes believed that the humble, or those who look to the City of God for their salvation, make the earthly regimes in which they live unstable. Their upward gaze makes them oblivious to the city of their residence—the one that matters most. Those who see themselves as humble servants of an otherworldly king doom the kingdoms of this world to interminable strife. Men thought to be possessed by greatness of soul, according to Hobbes, cannot be good citizens, subordinate to the state. Their swollen pride, or sense of honor, makes them ill-equipped for a new citizenship that is staked upon the idea of equality. While Hobbes thought his work would offer political salvation for all, magnanimous souls do not believe that they need to be saved.

In the biblical account of Job, God reminded Job of his mortality by invoking the name of the deep sea beast called the Leviathan. "King over all the sons of pride," the creature could not be controlled by human beings.[19] For Hobbes, an unconventional reader of Scripture, the story posed a particular challenge. Was it possible, he wondered, to construct a beast capable of taming the political pride that runs rampant in human beings? His book *Leviathan*, published in 1651, offered a blueprint for the beast's construction.

Just like Machiavelli, Hobbes had little time for the abstract formulations of ancient thinkers, pagan or Christian. Lampooning what he called the "Aristotelity" of his day, Hobbes also ridiculed the Christian influence on the politics of the day.[20] Most of all, he lamented the fact that Christianity, following Augustine's lead, had divided the political world into two opposing cities. This division, Hobbes held, was the real problem; the unity of political authority was the solution.

According to Hobbes, political confusion can be alleviated with the establishment of a single sovereign. Prior to the sovereign's rule, anything goes. There is nothing by nature right or wrong, good or evil. Moral categories only mean something when the political sovereign has been established. Sin is transgressing the law. By this argument, pride, or what we have called arrogance, is not sin but a political problem. Defined by Hobbes as thinking oneself unequal to others, pride is defined solely according to politics. Equality is not about rights, or dignity before God, or even standing on the same level before the law, but rather is defined according to man's equal vulnerability to violent attack and death. Pride pulls a man away from participation in the establishment of the sovereign by making him think he will be fine on his own. For that reason alone it is bad.

Humility in terms of obedience to God, or service to others, is irrelevant to Hobbes. All that matters is subservience before the political sovereign, the "mortal God," Leviathan, whose creation eliminates any confusion about two realms or cities or kingdoms.[21] All human life is orchestrated by the sovereign. Whereas for Augustine spiritual self-government is made possible by God's sovereignty, for Hobbes the spiritual world, such as it is, is ordered only when the political order is established. The salvation that mattered for Hobbes is political salvation, the avoidance of civil war. He was little concerned with spiritual regeneration. The opposite is true for Augustine, who saw no means of political salvation but every need for spiritual regeneration.

In Hobbes's estimation, both Augustine's humble Christian prince and Aristotle's magnanimous man would be terrible rulers and unwelcome citizens. The Christian prince sees God as sovereign and therefore would be a force for subversion, not cohesion. The magnanimous man, too, presumably would be unwilling to prostrate himself before Leviathan. His vainglory would keep him independent. For Hobbes, magnanimity is closer to madness than good rule. For the same reason that they would be terrible rulers, Augustine's Christian prince and Aristotle's magnanimous man would be bad citizens in Hobbes's ideal regime. Each is insufficiently compliant with its rigid constraints.

With his new secular political philosophy, Hobbes sought to make the problem of pride go away. Stripping pride of any natural or spiritual significance, and pushing God out of the picture altogether, Hobbes redefined the political temptation of pride so that the only solution that would work was his. Only a sovereign can save us!

As global exploration brought the New World into view of the old, new ideas about politics—and the place of political humility— also abounded. With John Locke, an Englishman who wrote his major political works only a decade after the death of Hobbes, came new awareness of the possibility of political regimes devoted to the guarantee of rights, including those of "life, liberty, and property." Taking some similar philosophical starting points as Hobbes, but coming to very different conclusions, Locke sketched a system of government that became, more than any other, the blueprint for America's Founders. In following Locke's lead on the pursuit of liberty as the end of good government, the Founders self-consciously rejected Hobbes.

For the Founders, Hobbes undermined the virtues that were necessary for good government and good citizenship. A nineteen-year-old Alexander Hamilton spoke for many when he inveighed against Hobbes by comparing him to the "Federal Farmer," a political opponent who in Hamilton's view had made an erroneous argument along the same lines as the Englishman. Addressing his political foe, Hamilton wrote that Hobbes "held, as you do, that he was, then perfectly free from all restraint of *law* and *government*. . . . And there is no virtue, but what is purely artificial, the mere contrivance of politicians. . . . But the reason he ran into this absurd and impious doctrine, was, that he disbelieved the existence of an intelligent superintending principle, who is the governor, and will be the final judge of the universe." For Hamilton, the error was decisive, for there is no moment in human history when man is a law unto himself. America was founded upon the fundamental truth of "a very dissimilar theory" to that propounded by Hobbes: an understanding of natural law ordained by God, the giver also of the reason by which human beings discern their natural rights.[22]

Aristotle and Augustine do not meet in a Machiavellian middle. Americans were no more amenable to the political ideas of Machiavelli than they were to those of Hobbes. The key was not creating a government in which a leader could feign goodness and get away with it, but rather in creating one in which goodness could not be counted on, but was nevertheless sought. If Augustine's humility represents a desire for moral goodness as called for in the Christian tradition, and Aristotle's magnanimity the quest for greatness of soul as defined by the classical tradition, we might say that America had a little of each in its founding. America's Founders knew the importance of humility and desired to be humble, but they also wished to make their mark. They were ambitious. They wanted to be great, but only if greatness came not at the expense of goodness.

Someone truly great will not be a glory-hog. And no one truly great can claim that he did everything in his life all on his own. On the contrary, the truly great person will be a servant. No less committed to excellence in everything, and still as dedicated to the highest achievements, the magnanimous man as servant can accomplish even more than when he tries to do it alone. Service is not servility. Meekness is not weakness. Humility is an essential part of true greatness of soul.

Each life of the five Americans featured next reveals the fact that humility and magnanimity can coexist in the same soul. The greatness of soul exemplified by these humble heroes is not the same as the Aristotelian virtue. Washington, Madison, Adams, Lincoln, and Douglass all lived with the temptation of pride. Their overcoming of these trials reveals to us the need for healthy pride as well as the hidden strength of humility.

PART II

TRIALS AND TEMPTATIONS

FOUR

GEORGE WASHINGTON

In a young nation enamored of republican Rome, no American was more frequently depicted as a Roman hero than George Washington. Lauded even during his lifetime as America's Cincinnatus, Washington was frequently depicted as the Roman general who rescued the republic, gave up his sword, and returned to his farm. Artists John Trumbull and Charles Willson Peale painted Washington as the retired warrior; the American general reveled in his Roman portrayal. Even before Washington assumed office as the first president of the United States, he was already regarded by his fellow citizens as great. Next to Washington, said American physician and patriot Benjamin Rush, every king in Europe would look like a valet. With a net worth topping $500 million in today's dollars, Washington was among the wealthiest men in America.[1] He was the best horseman in the land, and everywhere he went, the gallant, impeccably attired Virginian made a smashing appearance.

As one Pennsylvania newspaper gushed in 1777, "If there are spots in his character, they are like the spots in the sun, only discernible by the magnifying powers of a telescope. Had he lived in the days of idolatry, he would have been worshipped as a god."[2]

Given Washington's accomplishments—and the adulation that surrounded him while he was alive—how did he not end up with a swollen head? The answer lies in his acquired humility, hard earned over many decades. Prone to excessive pride, Washington also was tempted by vanity, concerned about his appearance, and guarded about his reputation. His humility eventually became a habit as he combated these temptations. Like much in his life, Washington acquired humility carefully, even methodically.

"MANFUL NOT SINFUL"

Washington's strong sense of self—today we might say self-esteem—was a constant throughout his life. So too was his temper, which was volcanic and regular in its eruptions. As a young man, Washington was cunning and even a little reckless. His early efforts at climbing the ladder of success sometimes seemed to be more about the gratification of his ego than the pursuit of the common good. Ignoring Washington's very real struggles, his hagiographer Parson Weems depicted a man of premade perfection. Other, later biographers have overemphasized Washington's self-serving attitude. As a result, they tend to miss Washington's awareness of his own faults, along with his struggle to overcome them. Writing in the mid-twentieth century, Douglas Southall Freeman claimed of Washington that he was "too zealously attentive to his prestige, his reputation and his popularity—too much the self-conscious national hero and too little the daring patriot."[3] A more recent biographer casts Washington as a relentless self-promoter, "madly ambitious and obsessed with recognition and renown."[4] In reality, George Washington had to struggle with vice in his day-to-day life as much as anyone else. An essential part of his greatness was his effectiveness in winning the ongoing battle against his own flaws, chief of which was his urge to aggrandize himself at the expense of others. Washington was not born humble any more than he was born great.

A product of his father Augustine Washington's second marriage, George wanted dearly to get beyond the middling societal position into which he was born. The sons from his father's first marriage had been given formal education. Though he did not receive such schooling, George nonetheless was a quick study in the practical arts of land surveying and exploration. An adventurous soul who thrilled to the prospect of glory on the battlefield, Washington joined the British army at the age of twenty and thereafter connived to rise in rank as fast as he could. "The young Washington," historian Ron Chernow writes, "could be alternately fawning and assertive, appealingly modest and distressingly pushy. While he knew the social forms, he could never quite restrain, much less conceal, the unstoppable force of his ambition."[5]

Restraint of unruly passions comes in self-government, a quality of soul that is the handiwork of humility. Sometimes portrayed as a stolid, even stony man, Washington in real life was a man of intense passions. His ability to rein them in has given us the impression today that he had none. As a twelve-year-old boy learning penmanship, George was introduced to a century-old Jesuit document, "The Rules of Civility and Decent Behavior in Company and Conversation." Copying the 110 rules carefully in his own hand, young Washington devoured the list. What he learned stuck with him throughout his life. "Strive not with your superior in argument, but always submit your judgment to others with modesty," read the fortieth rule. "Play not the peacock," began rule number fifty-four.[6] Many like this one were about sartorial matters, table manners, or other issues of decorum. What is notable about this list is how many of the rules related directly to modesty or humility. "Artificers and persons of low degree," went rule number thirty-six, "ought not to use many ceremonies to lords or others of high degree, but respect and highly honor them, and those of high degree ought to treat them with affability and courtesy, without arrogance."[7] This is one among many that urge the proper consideration of rank: respect those in higher positions than you, the Jesuits urged of all. To those in positions of authority they offered special advice: do not treat those lower than you in rank as if they are lowly. The central message that rings through to the reader is that one must humble himself before others, whatever their rank. The penultimate rule is short: "Let your recreations be manful not sinful." And the last one in the list is sublime in its simplicity: "Labor to keep alive in your breast that little spark of celestial fire called conscience."[8]

Ambition was tugging hard at George at the same time he was learning the "Rules." He was not from the lower ranks of plantation society, but he was not born into its elite either. He sought recognition from the landed and wealthy Virginians of his day, the same members of high society who admired his older half brother,

Lawrence. Some fourteen years George's senior, Lawrence became a hero of successful British army expeditions in Central and South America. Upon his homecoming, he married Anne Fairfax, of the immensely influential Virginia clan (her sister-in-law, Sally, was the later object of George's affection). Washington revered Lawrence and wanted a colonial American aristocratic lifestyle like his.

In this admiration of Lawrence, George revealed his desire for honor. The eighteenth-century French political thinker Montesquieu wrote of aristocrats in general, "[W]e are polite out of pride: we feel ourselves flattered by having manners that prove that we are not lower-class, and that we haven't lived among *that* sort of people."[9] In his early aspirations, there was some of this attitude in George Washington, for he defined himself as much according to what he was *not* as to what he was. His sense of honor—and dishonor—was intensely competitive, so much so that it rose to the level of what in early America was called "fame." Instead of connoting a love of notoriety that likely turns out to be fleeting, "fame" at the time of the founding referred to a more enduring quality—the longing for immortality based upon enduring accomplishment. As the historian Douglass Adair explains, fame in this sense is a kind of secular substitute for the Christian idea of eternal life.[10] The "love of fame," Alexander Hamilton wrote in the *Federalist*, "is the ruling passion of the noblest minds."[11]

Without ever having read the *Nicomachean Ethics*, Washington wanted to be Aristotle's magnanimous man. Washington's problem was that whereas the magnanimous man is great and knows he is great, Washington acted like he was great but was not yet so. In any rush to be great, it is easy to forget about goodness. In some of his early efforts to grab greatness, Washington lost sight of a goal higher than his own renown.

One such incident caused reverberations around the globe. In 1753, when Washington was only twenty-one and an adjutant general of the militia, Virginia's royal governor tasked him to lead a reconnaissance mission into the Ohio territory. Washington acquitted this duty ably and reported after his two-and-a-half-month trip into the wilderness that the French were encroaching on British-held soil and were making plans for further expansion. Paid a pittance for his strenuous labors and passed over for leadership of the expeditionary force that was subsequently assembled, Washington let his wounded pride lead the way in the actions that followed. Marching his small, ragtag band of colonists and Indians into a direct confrontation with a French force, Washington acted with a degree of rashness that resulted in the firing of the first shots of the French and Indian War. After this initial, violent exchange, Washington withdrew his men and then quickly fashioned a refuge in a large clearing called Great Meadows, outside of what is now Pittsburgh, Pennsylvania. His haste in choosing this open site led to the quick, July 4, 1754, surrender of what was dubbed Fort Necessity.

Washington learned from these painful early lessons. Of Washington's bravery no one ever expressed doubts. "I heard bullets whistle and believe me there was something charming in the sound," he recollected about his encounter with the French.[12] People did, however, question his braggadocio. Did his desire for renown cloud his judgment? On the heels of Washington's disastrous misadventure at Fort Necessity, the regiment he had led was divided into ten companies. Rather than take a demotion to the rank of captain of one of the ten, Washington quit. Deprived of a British royal commission, which would confer upon him the legitimacy he lacked as an American enlistee along with the promise of a lifelong career, Washington would volunteer for service eight months later. He did so in part because his wounded pride was partly salved by an offer from British major general Edward Braddock for him to become the general's aide-de-camp.

At this stage of Washington's life, Chernow notes, "his emotions were still raw, and he exhibited a naked, sometimes clumsy ambition that he later learned to cloak or conquer."[13] Washington's longing for the elusive British commission lingered, as did his desire to find a spouse who might further his financial goals. He was defeated in his first election effort, running unsuccessfully in 1755 for the Virginia House of Burgesses. It is one thing to want to change one's lot in life; it is another to be so eager to do so that the means of self-improvement do not matter. Greatness at any price is not real greatness. In Washington's early haste to achieve greatness, he sometimes let his ambition outpace his virtue. He gradually realized this, and he calibrated his actions accordingly. Rather than just cloaking his ambition, Washington recognized that the more he served others and the cause of justice, the more his success would matter. The less his ambition was about his own fame, the more he would deserve the honors he received. Virtue in this sense, he discovered, can be its own reward.

After some of his early struggles, we can see in hindsight an upward trajectory at every stage of Washington's life soon thereafter. In his inheritance of Mount Vernon upon the early deaths of his half brother and Lawrence's widow (the acquisition of which afforded Washington the same prestige and power he had envied in

Lawrence), his marriage to Martha Custis (which brought matrimonial joy, along with enormous wealth and plum social standing), his election victory to the House of Burgesses three years after he had lost, and his rise in military rank, we see all of the signs of an extraordinary ascent. The ultimate path of his trajectory at the time was not obvious to him. Nor was its attainment as easy as it might today seem. At every stage he was preoccupied with vexing questions. How should he prosecute the war against Great Britain while at the same time contending with plotters within his own ranks? Should he come out of retirement from the military and, putting his entire reputation on the line, attend the Constitutional Convention? Should he take the job, under the new Constitution, as the first president of the United States? Should he keep that job past the first two terms? In these and other critical decisions, it was not just Washington's reputation at stake, he came to realize, but the nation's success as well. They were decisions not just about his life; they affected a whole people. Keeping his pride in check was a matter of momentous consequence.

"THERE WAS A CHOICE OF DIFFICULTIES"

By the time colonial efforts at reconciliation with Great Britain looked impossible and armed conflict inevitable, George Washington had emerged as the overwhelming favorite to lead the American war effort. Selected by Congress in June 1775 to head the Continental Army, General Washington insisted that the Americans organize and train a standing army so that they would avoid a guerilla war with Great Britain. Despite endless trials in the training and provisioning of his forces, Washington galvanized an otherwise undistinguished army into an organized fighting force that enjoyed several critical early successes.

Almost from the outset of the Revolution, many Americans knew that their general possessed an immense power that could pose a danger to the republic. They feared this power in the abstract but trusted the man who wielded it. Abigail Adams, who knew Washington well, remarked about him, "[He] has so happy a faculty of appearing to accommodate and yet carrying his point that if he was really not one of the best-intentioned men in the world, he might be a very dangerous one."[14] Like Rome of old, America in its infancy saw the necessity of granting short-term powers of an extraordinary nature to a single person. The Roman term for this was *dictator*, and it carried for Romans none of the negative connotations it later (and deservedly) earned. Not just once but twice, Congress granted Washington the powers of a dictator: after the American collapse in New Jersey in November and December 1776, and then again in September 1777. Congress's grant of power was thoroughgoing, not just administrative. Twice Congress authorized Washington to "direct all things relative . . . to the operations of war."[15] Although there was no obligation under this grant of power for Washington to defer to Congress in any way, Washington continued to send along to Congress all of the matters it normally oversaw. He took under his purview only those matters where the state governing bodies were nonexistent or where they had been thrown into anarchy because of British disruption.

Two dictatorial actions by Washington, constitutional scholar

Glenn Phelps notes, drew the ire of some. Washington issued a loyalty oath requirement of citizens that he never enforced because of adverse reaction to it. He also enforced a timetable for farmers near the army's headquarters that regulated their planting and harvesting of grain. If they did not comply, their grain could be seized for use by the army.

At a moment of great temptation—when Washington could most easily have seized complete power over civilian and military affairs—he exercised the greatest restraint. What if Washington had given in to the temptation to seize absolute power? Washington could have taken Congress's grant of power as an invitation to take control of not just the military but much of society as well. Freezing out the ineffective state legislatures would have been easy, and while members of Congress would have raised a ruckus had Washington done so, the general could have done as many a dictator before him had and ignored the decrees of the national legislature or dissolved it altogether. Had he opted to claim absolute authority, Washington might then have followed the playbook of many previous dictators in claiming to speak and act on behalf of "the people." Operating the military "on their behalf" by accumulating more and more power, he could have also assumed control of the federal treasury, thereby taking over the power of taxation so as to increase the protection of "the people."

The Roman example was one many Americans knew. The idea was that a skilled leader would be installed for a set period of time, with the purpose of alleviating a crisis for which no other solution would work. Setting the term of dictatorship at six months, the Romans clearly defined the purpose of the dictatorship according to the crisis at hand. In Rome's degeneration from republic to empire, Julius Caesar cast aside all limitations of dictatorial authority as he gradually realized that he was becoming indispensable to the Roman people. Abandoning any pretense of humility before the law and tradition, Caesar sought and received the title *dictator perpetuo*, or "dictator for life," in February of 44 BC. The major question after that in Rome was whether there were enough freedom-loving souls who were willing to confront him. In Washington's time as general, a total of eight years, there was none of that slippery slope descent into tyranny. "It may seem a paradox that the chief advocate of a centralized professional army should also be the nation's most visible example of republicanism in action," Phelps writes. "Yet that is precisely what Washington's 'dictatorship' established."[16]

The fall of 1777 brought a couple of stinging defeats, and with the army unable to take back Philadelphia, it retreated to Valley Forge, Pennsylvania. "Viewing the subject in any point of light, there was a choice of difficulties," Washington wrote to the president of Congress from Valley Forge, in late December 1777.[17] If he tried to advance against the English too quickly, they could overwhelm the inferior forces of the Americans; if he tried to outlast them with defensive gambits, the American soldiers might lose heart. Success, let alone survival, was not inevitable.

In addition to the military bind, Washington was also under increasing political pressure. Because of the army's inability to control Philadelphia, the members of Congress had to relocate about a hundred miles away, to York, Pennsylvania. In Congress's new home, murmurings of George Washington's deficiencies became more frequent. As military historian Norman Gelb relates, Pennsylvania's attorney general said that Washington committed "such blunders as might have disgraced a soldier of three months' standing."[18] At the same time Washington's reputation was under attack, another military star was rising. At the Battle of Saratoga, in October 1777, General Horatio Gates won a smashing victory, the first significant success of the war. This prompted some in the states to grouse that Gates might be a better field general than Washington.

If George Washington had issued a blistering response to such congressional second-guessing, few would have been surprised. His main challenge was in keeping the army together at Valley Forge. The cold air was bitter, but so too was the attitude of many enlistees. They had signed up for duty with patriotic fervor, but when that sentiment gave way to the reality of the winter, many soldiers wanted to head home. Some eleven thousand men were at Valley Forge, and Washington needed every one of them.

Washington was worried about not just his enlisted ranks but also the ranks of officers who joined the army from overseas. With the addition of a number of foreign officers who had volunteered for American service came unexpected leaders like the Marquis de Lafayette, a French nobleman who became Washington's aide-de-camp, as well as unanticipated troublemakers like Thomas Conway, an Irish soldier from France. The high-stakes promotions process for such officers meant that they would jockey for position, some by publicly singing Washington's praises and others by privately criticizing his every move. Colonel Conway was in the latter camp, and for a while his whispers against General Washington caught the ears of some in Congress. Appointed in December 1777 to the congressional Board of War, Conway was joined on this important oversight committee by General Gates, who had been given the principal position on the committee. Conway wrote Gates of his desire to serve under Gates, not Washington, for "the more I see of [Washington's] army," Conway confided, "the less I think it fit for general action."[19]

In response, Gates did nothing to quell such insubordination; instead, he provoked it. When at his instigation the Board of War got congressional approval for a plan to chase the British into Canada, he did so without involving Washington. Rather than resign (which he briefly contemplated) or make recriminations against Conway and Gates, Washington worked to rally his men. He took swift action on the Conway Cabal, as it came to be called, notifying the Board of War about the malicious letter written by Conway to Gates, in which Conway complained about Washington's leadership. This action, which some historians have seen as overreaction, was mild compared to the alternatives. Washington could have taken the military dispute away from the civilian realm and wrested authority from Congress in order to settle the score with Gates and Conway. Or he could have quit, deciding that all of his appeals to Congress, back-channel politicking, and miserable scraping by at Valley Forge were beneath a man of his standing. Instead, he acted in deference to Congress and the rule of law and in the process strengthened the civilian control of the military.

The Americans' decisive defeat of the British army at Yorktown in October 1781 was followed by what seemed to early Americans a long period of wilderness wandering. During what turned out to be more than two years during which peace was negotiated and a treaty was ratified, Washington held that the army should not be disbanded. A standing army cannot stand on its accord, and while many of the merchants of New England were willing to pay the taxes necessary to support the soldiers, the appropriations and payment process required Washington's constant vigilance. An unpaid and unfed army is a restless army, and while Washington's troops did not go completely unpaid or unfed, congressional delays taxed the patience of the soldiers. All his men knew that Washington had never failed them. Why not make him king? For Washington, this idea was as wrongheaded as servility to the British monarch. It was a nonstarter, as a bold but reckless soul who proposed crowning Washington king would find out. In May 1782, American army colonel Lewis Nicola wrote General Washington to propose that Washington be made king. Washington rebuked this idea and wrote to Nicola, "Let me conjure you then, if you have any regard for your Country, concern for yourself or posterity, or respect for me, to banish these thoughts from your mind, and never communicate, as from yourself, or any one else, a sentiment of the like nature."[20] Nicola spent the rest of his life apologizing for his suggestion.

Six years after the long wilderness of Valley Forge, and eight years after the start of the War for Independence, General Washington announced his intention to give up his sword and return to civilian life. In a June 14, 1783, circular to the states, Washington addressed the significance of the war effort and the task that lay before the new nation. He acknowledged that such an ambitious rhetorical effort by a soon-to-be-retired general might be "ascribe[d] to arrogance or ostentation."[21] In fact, Washington spent most of the speech not laying out some grand national plan but rather imploring state leaders to pay their share of the troop salary and pensions. The "price of their blood and of your independency," Washington told the governors, while speaking of the soldiers, was a "debt of honour."[22] Washington closed his letter with a prayer— that citizens would live in a "spirit of subordination and obedience to government," and that God would "dispose us all, to do justice, to love mercy, and to demean ourselves with that charity, humility and pacific temper of mind, which were the characteristics of the Divine Author of our blessed religion, and without an humble imitation of whose example in these things, we can never hope to be a happy nation."[23] This statement was an almost direct quotation from the prophet Micah, who wrote, "He has showed you, O man, what is good; and what does the LORD require of you but to do justice, and to love kindness, and to walk humbly with your God?" (Mic. 6:8). Washington's prayer was not political propaganda or a nod to civil religion but a reminder of duties he shared with his fellow citizens.

"THE GREATEST MAN IN THE WORLD"

America in its earliest days had much about which to be humble. Seen as a lowly backwater by many elites of Britain and the European continent, it lacked the powerhouse intellectuals of France, the political pomp of monarchical courts, and the military might of Great Britain. The lowly colonies had something of real value, however, in the leadership of George Washington. Of the possibility that George Washington would relinquish his military power after a successful conclusion to America's War for Independence, British king George III said, "If he does, he will be the greatest man in the world."[24]

Washington was the greatest in large measure because of the humility he showed on December 23, 1783. On that day, at noon, in Annapolis, Maryland, the seat of the young nation's national legislature, General Washington resigned his military commission. His journey to Annapolis was long and winding, but Washington's address to Congress was short. Its six paragraphs marked the establishment of the civilian control of the military and the surrender of military might to popular self-government.

"Mr. President," the general began, addressing the head of Congress, "the great events on which my resignation depended having at length taken place; I have now the honor of offering my sincere congratulations to Congress and of presenting myself before them to surrender into their hands the trust committed to me, and to claim the indulgence of retiring from the service of my country." As was typical of his public pronouncements about the leading roles he assumed throughout the young nation's early years, Washington emphasized that he took the job with "diffidence" that "was superseded by a confidence in the rectitude of our cause, the support of the supreme power of the Union, and the patronage of heaven."[25] Before his concluding resignation, Washington offered gratitude to his officers, to "the interposition of Providence," and to his "countrymen."[26]

Washington's resignation speech hit many of the same notes as did a letter he wrote to the leadership of the Reformed German congregation of New York in late November 1783. Noting the difficulties that had been overcome in the American struggle, Washington acknowledged the thanks he had received from the church elders. "And if my humble exertions have been made in any degree subservient to the execution of the divine purposes," Washington wrote, "a contemplation of the benediction of heaven on our righteous cause, the approbation of my virtuous countrymen, and the testimony of my own conscience, will be a sufficient reward and augment my felicity beyond anything which the world can bestow."[27]

Washington identified his cause as "the establishment of civil and religious liberty."[28] He was instrumental in this cause; his exertions were not meager. Washington himself knew these things. So why would he call his efforts "humble"? Was this false humility? For a man of action, deeds matter more than words. "Deeds, not words" was one of his mottos, his step-granddaughter reported.[29] When he did speak, Washington was quick to extend credit to others. When he invoked Providence, Washington did so hesitatingly, never with the jingoism that marked political diatribes and numerous pulpit sermons of the day. Acutely aware of his reputation, keen on accomplishment, and ambitious for action, Washington gave himself to the well-being of those he called the "unborn millions."[30] As he concluded his resignation speech:

> I consider it an indispensable duty to close this last solemn act of my official life, by commending the interests of our dearest country to the protection of Almighty God, and those who have the superintendence of them, to his holy keeping. Having now finished the work assigned me, I retire from the great theater of action; and bidding an affectionate farewell to this august body under whose orders I have so long acted, I here offer my Commission, and take my leave of all the employments of public life.[31]

In a draft of his speech, Washington had used the terms "final farewell" and "ultimate leave." In scratching *final* and *ultimate*, Washington left the door open for entry into future public service. Upon his speech's conclusion, historian Stanley Weintraub notes, Washington pulled from his coat pocket the parchment on which his congressional appointment as commander in chief was written. Dated June 15, 1775, the paper was symbolic of the sword he had wielded so effectively. In leaving it behind in the hands of Congress, General Washington, First Soldier, became George Washington, citizen.[32]

"HIS HIGH MIGHTINESS"

When America's Founders had to figure out the formal title for the newly created position of president, one proposal was especially unhumble: "His High Mightiness, the President of the United States and Protector of Their Liberties." For one august American, George Washington, that title might have been apt. But as the congressional committee in charge of the matter finally decided, the title had to be simpler—more American. Their solution stuck, as we still refer directly to our head of state as "Mr. President." While Washington himself flirted with the loftier proposal, ultimately he came to the same opinion as the committee: the president was not a monarch, and his title should not be like a king's.

Had George Washington opted for the more exalted title, abolished the naming committee, dissolved Congress, and taken office for life, it would have been less surprising than what actually happened. Without General Washington, there would have been no victory in the War for Independence. Without victory, no nation. Without a nation, no government. And without a government, no head of state. The very office Washington first occupied owed its existence, in large measure, to his labor.

The delegates to the Constitutional Convention in Philadelphia knew this. Even before they convened their meeting in May 1787, Washington's welcome—complete with the sounds of cannon fire and church bells—befitted a head of state.[33] When the delegates debated the contentious topic of what the new chief executive should look like (under the Articles of Confederation there was no such position), all the delegates knew that the man presiding over the Convention would also be elected to the office that was to be created in the Constitution.

Washington knew it too. In his copy of the Constitution, the only marginal notes he made are those related to the powers of the president.[34] And yet he never acted like a demagogue. On the contrary, he knew that if the Constitutional Convention were to be successful, the nation would have to rely upon him less and upon the people more. "The happiness of this country," George Washington wrote in private correspondence at the start of the Constitutional Convention, "depends much upon the deliberations of the federal Convention which is now sitting. It, however, can only lay the foundation—the community at large must raise the edifice."[35] Acknowledging the importance of the efforts under way in Philadelphia, Washington knew in the early goings that in structuring a representative form of government, the delegates were creating a regime in which the people were ultimately responsible for its success.

Although as president of the Convention, Washington could have intervened whenever he wanted to over the course of the four months of deliberations, he did so infrequently, speaking on a substantial matter only once. On the Convention's last day, when a motion was made to change the ratio of representation for the proposed U.S. House of Representatives, Washington spoke in favor of the change to a greater number of representatives and thus a lower ratio of constituents to representatives in each of the nation's congressional districts. Sending an olive branch to those who doubted the wisdom of the larger constitutional plan that was about to be adopted, Washington also underscored his support for republican— or representative—government, the core idea of the new American form of government. With Washington's support, the motion passed unanimously.[36]

Washington knew that the real struggle for the Constitution would start after the Convention adjourned on September 17, 1787. The states were set to debate the ratification of the document, and while it would go into effect if nine of the thirteen states approved it, it would only be secure in its enactment if the large states of New York, Massachusetts, and Virginia joined. As much as many Americans looked forward to Washington assuming office as the first president of the United States, Washington was careful not to do anything to short-circuit the more than two-year process of ratification. Speaking of Washington's assuming the office almost as a *fait accompli*, Alexander Hamilton wrote Washington a month after New York's July 1788 ratification to express his anticipation of Washington's election as president. Rather than plotting with Hamilton how this might happen or reveling in the prospect,

Washington expressed his love of Mount Vernon and his life in retirement. "I hope I shall always possess," Washington wrote, "firmness and virtue enough to maintain (what I consider the most enviable of all titles) the character of an honest man, as well as prove (what I desire to be considered in reality) that I am."[37] Washington wanted the job of president. He was ambitious for it. But his humility in this letter and his actions were not false, for they were marked by an honesty that meant he subordinated his self-interest to higher ends. Washington's humility before the law and the Constitution elevated his ambition.

"TO ALL LIBERTY OF CONSCIENCE"

In response to the first presidential election under the Constitution, which resulted in Washington's unanimous electoral victory, letters of congratulations poured in from across the country. Religious denominations in particular took delight in extending their good wishes and benedictions. To each of these congregations— Protestant, Catholic, and Jewish—Washington responded with much the same message. Thanking them profusely for their kind words, President Washington went on to assure his correspondents, many of whom had suffered persecution in other countries and thus were especially grateful for the religious liberty bestowed in America, that in the United States they could practice their faith as a matter of right, not privilege. "No one," he wrote to Baptists from Virginia, "would be more zealous than myself to establish effectual barriers against the horrors of spiritual tyranny, and every species of religious persecution."[38] Religious liberty is essential to civil liberty, and without civil liberty there is no liberty at all. In America, religious liberty was universal, Washington wrote. For the state to protect their rights, the religiously minded must also uphold good government. They must be citizens—zealous not only of their own rights but also those of others.

The lesson he taught his fellow citizens in his letters to religious bodies was that of submission to the law and to the Constitution. Submission, but also protection. If you obey the law, the law will protect you. Washington's implacable defense of religious liberty demonstrates that even if he did not formally hold the title "Protector of Their Liberties," as had been proposed by Congress for the president, he earned it. No body of religious believers saw that more clearly than the Hebrew Congregation of Newport, Rhode Island.

Recalcitrant "Rogue Island" was the last state of the original thirteen to ratify the Constitution, but once the state finally did so, in 1790, its citizens earned a presidential visit from George Washington. On August 18 of that year, a group of Newport notables greeted Washington by reading to him a hearty round of letters. Moses Seixas, the Newport congregation's warden, or lay assistant, read his synagogue's letter aloud. Addressing the president as "Sir" and saluting his "merits" at the outset of their missive, the congregation noted that they had been "deprived ... of the invaluable rights of free citizens." It was with "a deep sense of gratitude to the Almighty disposer of all events" that they "behold a government, erected by the majesty of the people—a government, which to bigotry gives no sanction, to persecution no assistance," and instead gives "to all liberty of conscience." Thanking "the Ancient of Days" for "all these blessings of civil and religious liberty," they recognized that this divine gift can be realized by citizens only if the government is up to the task of guaranteeing it.[39] God gives it, but good government ensures that liberty is not reserved for the favored few.

President Washington's response to the congregation, sent three days after he had received their letter to him, quoted liberally from their original missive. Washington's salutation was significant, if easily overlooked, for in addressing the members of the congregation simply as "gentlemen" and referring to "all classes as citizens," the president accorded recognition to them as fellow Americans, not strangers in his land. "It is no more that toleration is spoken of as if it were by the indulgence of one class of people that another enjoyed the exercise of their inherent natural rights," Washington wrote. The United States, he added, "which gives to bigotry no sanction, to persecution no assistance, requires only that they who live under its protection should demean themselves as good citizens in giving it on all occasions their effectual support." And then, in conclusion, Washington offered his fellow citizens a closing benediction drawn in part from Micah: "May the children of the stock of Abraham, who dwell in this land, continue to merit and enjoy the good will of the other inhabitants; while every one shall sit in safety under his own vine and fig tree, and there be none to make him afraid."[40]

"Conscience," Washington learned as a young man in writing out the "Rules for Civility," is a "little spark of celestial fire." One must "labor" to keep it "alive."[41] Knowing that he was not the creator of his conscience but rather its keeper, he maintained a vigilant regard for doing what was right. Washington knew that both in his own life and in that of the nation he loved, a firm reliance upon the divine was necessary. As he stated in his Farewell Address, "Of all the dispositions and habits which lead to political prosperity, religion and morality are indispensable supports."[42]

Washington's faith in God was not that of a man who believed in a remote cosmic force, detached from a world wound up and left to tick on its own accord. Nor was his faith merely a civil religion where the intoning of pieties would placate the religious and produce the right political effect. Rather, the evidence from Washington's life points to the fact that he held regard for a God who was active in the lives of human beings and of nations. "The great Lord and Ruler of Nations,"[43] as Washington referred to God, was also, he stated, "the Divine Author of our blessed Religion."[44] Washington needed the Almighty to overcome the temptations he faced. He also knew that without submission before "the Judge of the Hearts of Men," neither he nor the nation would succeed.[45] For Washington, religion was vital to the health of human souls—and the body politic.

"THE HIGHEST AMBITION OF EVERY AMERICAN"

After serving as president for two four-year terms, George Washington could have sought reelection to a third term, as the Constitution at that time did not specify a term limit. Instead of trying for a third term, Washington opted to retire. He was thought to be indispensable because he knew he was not. As he stated in 1789, "It should be the highest ambition of every American to extend his views beyond himself, and to bear in mind that his conduct will not only affect himself, his country, and his immediate posterity; but that its influence may be co-extensive with the world, and stamp political happiness or misery on ages yet unborn."[46]

From Washington's installation as general of the Continental Army on June 15, 1775, until his December 23, 1783, resignation from that role, he had been on the job a total of 3,114 days. During that time he was able to return to his beloved Mount Vernon for only two brief visits—for a strategy session in 1781 with French general Rochambeau and later that same year to comfort his wife, Martha, upon the death of her last surviving child from her first marriage. While serving as president, Washington could return more often to Mount Vernon, but with the capital of the young country in New York City, and then Philadelphia, hundreds of miles away, his visits were far less frequent than he wished. With his public work finally completed in 1797, Washington retired to Mount Vernon. His career established the American precedent that no person, including the president, is above the laws and the Constitution. Over the course of his life he learned that fame would be worthless if achieved for the wrong reasons. His ambition, above all else, was to act justly for the sake of others and his country. This did not mean that he always succeeded. Washington was ambitious, but his was not an arrogant—or "pushful"—ambition.[47] Rather, to use a term from the "Rules of Civility," it was "manful."[48]

In January 1800, a month after George Washington's death, a Baptist minister named Henry Holcombe paid tribute to Washington in a sermon that became known throughout the land. Calling Washington the "greatest of men," Holcombe noted that "an essential part of his honor was humility. He had as little of that tumid pride, which in its plentitude goes before destruction, as any man on earth." His "boldness and magnanimity," Holcombe said, were "equaled by nothing but his modesty and humility."[49] In choosing twice to leave power when he could have stayed at its pinnacle, George Washington earned the title "American Cincinnatus."

FIVE

JAMES MADISON

The man who would earn the title "Father of the Constitution" was the first out-of-state delegate to arrive in Philadelphia for the May 1787 Constitutional Convention. The man who was "Father of His Country" almost didn't make it. Without James Madison's intensive lobbying of George Washington in advance of the proceedings, the senior Virginian might have opted to sit out the meeting.

When Washington arrived in The City of Brotherly Love for the Constitutional Convention, Philadelphians feted him as a hero. There was no such welcome committee for Madison, who arrived eight days earlier than Washington. Nor was there any grand hoopla on the Convention's scheduled start date of May 14, 1787. There wasn't even a quorum. As Madison stood with Washington in the Philadelphia State House, nearly a foot shorter than the retired general, we can only wonder what words were exchanged between the two men. Mortified at how many delegates were missing, and worried about whether the meeting in Philadelphia would fail for lack of attendance, as had the meeting in Annapolis, Maryland, eight months before, Madison might have muttered something like he later wrote to Thomas Jefferson—that there was "less punctuality in the outset than was to be wished."[1] Had Washington been concerned mainly about keeping his sterling reputation, he might have hightailed it out of town when he discovered that no one but Madison and a few Pennsylvanians had bothered to be on time. Instead, he waited for more delegates to arrive. "These delays," he wrote in a May 20 letter, "sour the temper of the punctual members."[2] Taking advantage of the extra time, Madison led daily meetings with his fellow Virginians to lay the groundwork for what would be an all-out assault on the Articles of Confederation.

"PIGMY"

The Convention finally convened on Friday, May 25. After his unanimous election as president of the Convention, Washington was given a high-backed chair in the front of the room. Madison seated himself at the front of the room, where he could face the Convention president, keep up with all of the action, and offer his own contributions to the debate. Seated near each other, Madison and Washington had to have struck the other fifty-three delegates who participated in the Convention as an especially odd pair of collaborators.

As skilled socially as he was brave on the battlefield,

Washington commanded the attention of all who were near him by his physical presence alone. Madison's aura, however, was pale and sickly. A hypochondriac from his youth, Madison suffered from several actual illnesses and maladies over the course of his eighty-five years of life. Some of his poor health was a result of his own doing, as he exhausted himself through overwork. Standing five feet three inches in height and weighing just shy of one hundred pounds, Madison was slight of frame. Described by one Federalist critic as a "pigmy," he possessed few of the social skills that might otherwise compensate for his unimpressive physical presentation.[3] Reticent to engage others at large social occasions, Madison warmed up some in smaller settings, but even then he could betray an awkwardness that, especially during his bachelor days, was off-putting. (He married the vivacious widow Dolley Payne Todd later in life, when he was forty-three and she was twenty-six.) Even in legislative assemblies, where one might guess he would shine, Madison was underwhelming. His loquacity at the Convention was not to be confused with oratorical accomplishment, for in assemblies in which he served throughout his over forty-year political career, Madison's colleagues complained about the hesitancy of his speech and how hard it was even to hear the voice of their diminutive colleague.

Madison's physical size was indicative to some who encountered him of a small-minded rigidity and debilitating hesitancy or indecision. Even after Madison's prodigious labors at the Constitutional Convention and his election to the U.S. House of Representatives from Virginia, some still saw Madison as unfit for leadership. "His mildness of character and a certain timidity which accompanies his political conduct render him unfriendly to a republican government," South Carolina congressman William L. Smith complained in 1789.[4] New Englander Federalist Fisher Ames, a leading opponent of Madison, admitted that the Virginian had expert knowledge of political affairs. Despite this fact, Madison was "a little too much of a book politician, and too timid in his politics, for prudence and caution are opposites of timidity." Ames later added that Madison "seems evidently to want manly firmness and energy of character."[5]

In commenting on Madison's perceived weakness, his critics sometimes used the term *meek*. As William Constable, former aide-de-camp to the Marquis de Lafayette, wrote in July 1789 to his business partner, Gouverneur Morris—a leading voice in the Constitutional Convention—just as the first Congress was about to convene, "Many wish you were in the House of Representatives to lead; Madison is too meek to govern."[6] Later, when Madison was serving as Jefferson's secretary of state, one of his adversaries within his political party, Virginian John Randolph, indicted "the weak, feeble and pusillanimous spirit of the keeper of the Cabinet."[7]

For Aristotle, pusillanimity is to magnanimity what cowardice is to courage—a deficiency that falls short of the virtue. A pusillanimous man, Aristotle explained, possesses too little self-worth, or "too low" an opinion of himself, "whether his worth is great or moderate or little." He lives below his ability and beneath the "advantages that he deserves."[8] Compared to vanity, which is the excess of magnanimity, pusillanimity is a worse vice, for while a vain man will foolishly undertake large tasks for which he is unprepared, the pusillanimous man will not even take up large tasks. In the hurly-burly of political life, this diffidence amounts to paralysis.

As Thomas Hobbes wrote of it, "Pusillanimity disposeth men to irresolution, and consequently to lose the occasions, and fittest opportunities of action."[9]

"CHRISTIAN MAGNANIMITY"

Before Madison ever launched a career of any kind, and just after college, he seemed incapable of taking up the smallest task, let alone large ones. Born in 1751, the eldest of twelve children, Jemmy, or Junior, as he was called, was well off as a child and never wanted for money throughout his life. His father owned more than three thousand acres in Orange County, Virginia, near the Blue Ridge Mountains, which made him the county's top landowner. As such, James Madison Sr. was happy to support his son's scholarly pursuits. From the start, Junior excelled in his schoolwork. Tutored at home until he was eleven, he spent most of his adolescence seventy miles away from home studying and boarding with a Scottish tutor. At the age of eighteen, James traveled three hundred miles by horse-back, together with his tutor at the time and a family slave, to the College of New Jersey, now Princeton University.

Madison flourished in his collegiate studies. Rote memoriza-tion marked most college-level instruction, but at the College of New Jersey, President John Witherspoon had instituted changes that resulted in much more give-and-take in the classroom. The cur-riculum was still classical and oriented to the training of Christian ministers, but the inquiry was more free and the deliberation among faculty and students more lively. Witherspoon's wish for the school was that the "spirit of liberty [which breathes] high and strong" would prevail.[10] He insisted that the college's goal was not to "dictate with an air of infallibility," but rather to put students on the path to truth.[11] The only clergyman to sign the Declaration of Independence, the Reverend Dr. Witherspoon instilled in his students the same passion he showed for public service. College president from 1768 through his death in 1794, Witherspoon rebuilt the main building, Nassau Hall, where Madison lived while on campus, after it was overrun by British troops in the Revolutionary War's Battle of Princeton. Woodrow Wilson, Princeton's president in the first decade of the twentieth century, called the college under Witherspoon "a seminary of statesmen."[12] More than seventy members of the United States Congress and three Supreme Court justices, among many other high office holders, were Witherspoon's students.

James Madison was at the head of that illustrious class. An outstanding student, Madison's facility with foreign languages served him well (Greek and Latin were required; French and Italian were his own pursuits). He was a voracious reader and digested with ease the writings of thinkers imported by Witherspoon from Scotland (David Hume, Francis Hutcheson, and Thomas Reid were introduced to Americans in large measure via Witherspoon). The "old Doctor," as Madison fondly remembered him, taught the young scholar the place of moral as well as intellectual virtue. Witherspoon warned against excess pride, noting that "nothing more certainly makes a man ridiculous than an over-forwardness to display his excellencies."[13] Human beings are fallen, Madison heard many times from Witherspoon, but they are not so fallen that they are incapable of self-government. As Madison biographer Ralph Ketcham has pointed out, Witherspoon taught all of his students, including Madison, that "the purpose of government was to encourage and nourish not life alone but the good life, the life of virtue."[14]

Among the virtues Witherspoon wished to see revived in American life was magnanimity. Specifically, Witherspoon wanted to resuscitate the idea of "Christian magnanimity" against the critique of Christianity leveled by the eighteenth-century Scottish philosopher David Hume. In a sermon Witherspoon first preached in 1775, just three years after Madison had departed Princeton, he described the view he was combating: "Some infidels have in terms affirmed that Christianity has banished magnanimity and by its precepts of meekness, humility, and passive submission to injury has destroyed that nobleness of sentiment which rendered the ancients so illustrious and gives so much majesty and dignity to the histories of Greece and Rome."[15] Echoing Augustine, Witherspoon claimed that Christians are well-suited for withstanding hard times and achieving great things, for they have help from on high. Human beings are equal before God, "for we must all appear before the judgment seat of Christ."[16] (They are also equal before God, he otherwise emphasized, because they are "endowed by their Creator" with natural rights, in the words of the Declaration of Independence Witherspoon signed.)[17] The prospect of divine judgment should humble all human beings and goad them to greatness for the sake of God's glory.

Whether Madison heard an early version of this sermon in one of Witherspoon's seminars on moral philosophy is unknown, but Madison did opt to stay on beyond his graduation for six months, reading Hebrew with Witherspoon and otherwise devoting himself to the life of the mind. Not inclined to a career in ministry or in the law, Madison pursued all his studies, it appeared, out of an intense interest in learning for its own sake. Having tested out of the first half of the curriculum at the College of New Jersey, Madison completed his undergraduate degree in two years, not the usual four. In his informal postgraduate work, he studied himself into a state of exhaustion.

"THE FULL AND FREE EXERCISE OF RELIGION"

At the age of twenty-one, in 1772, Madison returned to the family home, Montpelier, suffering from a debilitating *ennui*. His early life funk left him indecisive about everything of importance. To his best friend from college, William Bradford, who went on to become the second attorney general of the United States, Madison admitted of himself that he was "too dull and infirm now to look out for any extraordinary things in this world." He added that he did not "expect a long or healthy life" and that he had "little spirit and alacrity to set about any thing that is difficult in acquiring and useless in possessing after one has exchanged time for eternity."[18]

In his dejected state of mind, Madison was unable to see how well his makeup and education had prepared him for a career in politics. Just as the body of a world-class runner looks as if it is built for speed, Madison's intellectual form was fitted perfectly for legislative politics. His physical presence might have been anemic, but his political presence, developed over time, was strong. His political modus operandi never relied upon overawing power, rhetorical pyrotechnics, or charismatic cajolery. Rather, his way was thorough: study, share the results of your studies, and get ahead of the debate to come. Anticipation and timing are the fast-twitch muscles of political work, and Madison succeeded over and over again in knowing where to be before the moment of political need had arisen. By the time he left politics, he had served in elective office for more than thirty years. His race was an ultra-marathon, not a sprint.

Madison emerged from his post-collegiate dysphoria in the early days of the American Revolution. In 1774, the year of the Boston Tea Party, Madison was elected to the Orange County Committee of Safety. Because of his father's leadership of the county's militia, Junior received a commission as colonel. It was only a title, as Madison's fickle constitution precluded his service (he would much later ride into battle during the War of 1812). In April 1776, Madison was elected to travel to Williamsburg to represent Orange County at the Virginia Provincial Convention, which was to take the place of the defunct royal government. In addition to passing a unanimous recommendation of American independence on to the Continental Congress, the Convention set out to create a Declaration of Rights for the Commonwealth of Virginia. Madison was among the nearly three dozen members of the committee charged with this task.

Historian Jack Rakove has noted that Madison found his life's calling in the work of this convention, for it was there he started to discover politics as a "vocation."[19] As Virginians sought to extricate their state from its historic ties to the British Empire, passions ran high about the Anglican church establishment. From an early age, Madison had been outraged by the Anglicans' tyrannical treatment of Baptists in Virginia, particularly in Culpeper County, adjacent to

Orange County. Forced to pay for a church of which they were not members, Baptists in his area—and around the state—also were prevented from worshiping or proselytizing as they pleased and punished if they violated the ban. For Madison, the harassment and abuse they endured were an offense against civil and religious liberty that struck at the very heart of republican government.

In Williamsburg, Colonel George Mason, a hero of the American Revolution, drafted the first version of the Virginia Bill of Rights. His statement on religious liberty was pegged to the idea of toleration, a Lockean notion that was popular in England and the colonies. Characterizing religion as "the duty which we owe to our Creator," Mason's draft insisted that "only by reason and conviction, not by force or violence," can that duty be discharged. "Therefore," it continued, "all men should enjoy the fullest toleration in the exercise of religion, according to the dictates of conscience."[20]

Immediately upon seeing Mason's draft, Madison saw the opportunity for amendment. One part of his proposal seemed minor, but in fact it was momentous: change "toleration," he suggested, to "full and free exercise." Baptists and anyone else thereby would not need to rely upon the majority's goodwill but could worship more freely, confident that the state would protect their God-given right to religious liberty. Excited by the possibilities of systemic reform, Madison introduced more comprehensive language that went far beyond Mason's and would have resulted in the effective disestablishment of the Anglican church by making illegal its state-mandated, taxpayer-provided financial support. This move had no chance of passing because of the antidisestablishmentarianism represented by Patrick Henry, the powerful, eloquent legislator and later multi-term governor, and his allies. (Henry and his allies never used that word, one of the longest in the English language, probably for good reason.) Even though the final version of the legislation did not disestablish the Anglican church, it did result in an end to the prosecutions of religious believers and many dissenters. Even more, it put Virginia's religious and political establishment on notice that they would have to contend with a new and forceful opponent. In its final form, Article XVI of the June 1776 Virginia Declaration of Rights stated:

> That Religion, or the duty we owe our Creator, and the manner of discharging it, can be directed only by reason and conviction, not by force or violence; and, therefore, all men are equally entitled to the free exercise of religion, according to the dictates of conscience; and that it is the mutual duty of all to practice Christian forbearance, love, and charity, towards each other.[21]

Madison's successful insistence that no sovereign can rule over the human conscience was a landmark moment in the history of religious liberty. For him, it was just a start.

"IF MEN WERE ANGELS"

In the decade between the signing of the Declaration of Independence and the run-up to the Philadelphia Convention, Madison's life was a swirl of legislative activity. As the new nation was born, Madison came of age politically. On July 5, 1776, he celebrated America's independence by joining in the unanimous vote of the

Virginia Convention in favor of the resolution for independence. The impact of independence was immediate and felt in ways both small and large. No longer would "God save the King" be required in Anglican church services. Nor would Americans think of themselves as subjects. Now they were citizens.

In 1778 and 1779, Madison served as one of eight members of the Governor's Council of Virginia, where his diligence in wartime work earned him a position representing Virginia in Congress. At the age of twenty-nine, Madison was the youngest member of the Continental Congress. His next three years of work in Philadelphia laboring under the deficiencies of the Articles of Confederation revealed to Madison the problem of legislative or majority tyranny. States had too much power; when the national government needed to get something done in service of the whole people, it had no authority to do so. Majorities in each state legislature were preventing the nation from progressing toward real liberty. In thinking about the protection of liberty and the advancement of equality, Madison did not automatically assume that local or state governments were the best guarantors of human flourishing. Too often tyranny finds its best enforcers, he believed, at the local or state level. A democratic majority could be as fearsome a tyrant as a single despot.

Another important aspect of Madison's political thought came together as a result of his experience in Congress under the Articles of Confederation. Madison's study of the history of confederacies— spurred on by his experience operating in one—allowed him to see that their growth in population, territory, and economic productivity would be stunted by their lack of a strong central authority. Athens at the time of Socrates was a city of some 250,000 people, including slaves; it was democratic in its form of government, as citizen votes dictated many of its policies. Its problem was that in subjecting major decisions to the direct vote of citizens, it ceded too much authority to the passions of the people. Madison wrote, "Had every Athenian citizen been a Socrates, every Athenian assembly would still have been a mob."[22] Factions, or passionate majorities or minorities who act against the common good, flourish in a purely democratic form of government. Factions also exist in republican government, where the people rule indirectly through representatives, but their ill effects were more easily combated. Direct democracy, Madison maintained, was dangerous because of the greater likelihood of majority tyranny. Republican government was also dangerous for the same reason but less so.

What could be done about the danger? Madison's answer was one of the most innovative political theories ever advanced. The first option, he offered in *Federalist* 10 as an unrealistic foil, is to get rid of the danger. No matter the form of government, he explained, factions are inevitable. They form as a result of differences in people, and people are unequal in wealth, ability, or religious opinions. To get rid of factions is to get rid of liberty; that is not a viable option. Alternatively, and equally unrealistically, everyone could be given the same opinions. That option is as undesirable as quashing liberty. Government is supposed to protect the diversity of faculties, not destroy them. As Madison wrote, "The latent causes of faction are thus sown in the nature of man."[23]

For Madison, the nature of man is fundamentally prideful, even arrogant. Human beings are self-interested creatures, bent upon their own advancement, often at the expense of their fellows.

In theological terms, they are fallen; in political vocabulary, they are fallible. Madison's most famous words capture this: "But what is government itself but the greatest of all reflections on human nature? If men were angels, no government would be necessary." If angels governed mankind, all might be well. But since that is not the case, human beings have to devise political arrangements for the fact that all men, including politicians, are not perfect. As Madison put it, "In framing a government which is to be administered by men over men, the great difficulty lies in this: you must first enable the government to control the governed; and in the next place oblige it to control itself." Establishing this control without imperiling liberty is most difficult. "A dependence on the people is, no doubt, the primary control on the government; but experience has taught mankind the necessity of auxiliary precautions."[24]

The constant temptation for politicians is that they will let the possibility of present benefits—those they dole out and those they receive—crowd out all other thinking. A statesman, it has been said, thinks about future generations, while the politician thinks about his own. This is a false dichotomy. Politics is not disinterested. Politicians certainly are not. They are people like everyone else, combating the same tendency to self-aggrandize. Madison's challenge was to figure out how self-interest and self-government could coexist. His solution was to recognize that self-interest could not be banished from government but should be made a part of it. "Ambition must be made to counteract ambition," he concluded.[25] A republic should be large in size, so that as factions multiply, there are more to offset each other. No one faction will dominate. Direct democracy is dangerous, but old-fashioned small republicanism—where the presumption was that popular virtue alone could sustain the polity—was not much better. The American republic had to be large, and its government had to be arranged so that the formation of majority factions is difficult. To achieve this, "auxiliary precautions" are necessary—the separation of powers, checks and balances, federalism, and the other constitutional constraints like enumerated powers that protect the liberty of the people.[26]

Madison's political philosophy might look as if it is built on distrust of the citizens it is designed to protect. The world he supposes—full of clever, cunning, "pushful" people—seems inhospitable, even depressing. As the political scientist Richard K. Matthews has written, "Madison has little faith in either the demos or virtue" (*demos* is Greek for the masses).[27] In fact, Madison did not lack faith in people or virtue but in the wrong combination of popular passions and political arrangements. His groundbreaking political theory was that people could be trusted with self-government if the right structural protections were put into place. "The aim of every political constitution is, or ought to be, first to obtain for rulers men who possess most wisdom to discern, and most virtue to pursue, the common good of the society," he said, "and in the next place, to take the most effectual precautions for keeping them virtuous whilst they continue to hold their public trust."[28]

Virtue, though unreliable, is vital. As Madison wrote, "As there is a degree of depravity in mankind which requires a certain degree of circumspection and distrust, so there are other qualities in human nature which justify a certain portion of esteem and confidence. Republican government presupposes the existence of these qualities in a higher degree than any other form."[29] While Madison's mention of "depravity" sounds a lot like his Calvinist teacher at the College of New Jersey, John Witherspoon, Madison did not give up on his fellow citizens because they were fallen. Because all human beings are fallible, government must be more humble about its aims.

"AN ARROGANT PRETENSION"

With the adoption of Article XVI of the Virginia Bill of Rights having failed to disestablish the Anglican church in 1776, Madison and Jefferson sought another opportunity to take up that cause. In 1777, Jefferson drafted the "Bill for Establishing Religious Freedom." He formally introduced it in the legislature in 1779, only to see it languish, unconsidered, more than five years later. Stating that all people, including political rulers, are "but fallible and uninspired men," the bill affirmed the fact that "Almighty God hath created the mind free."[30] Fallible but free, human beings are not the creatures of the state; their consciences cannot be controlled by political forces. The Anglican church should be divested of its illegitimate authority; Virginians should be freed from the burden of its financial support and the tyranny of its imposition.

For Patrick Henry, the problem in Virginia was not too much support for the state religion but too little. To halt what he saw as the recent decline in public and private morality, Henry proposed a bill in 1784 that would establish funding for teachers of Christianity in Virginia. To be funded by a general assessment, or tax, Henry's bill argued that the public support of religion was necessary for popular virtue to thrive. Swayed by the prudential regard for the promotion of virtue, George Washington, future Supreme Court Chief Justice John Marshall, and well-regarded Virginia politician Richard Henry Lee all supported the bill. With Jefferson in France, the duty to defend religious liberty fell to Madison, who in 1784 was serving his second stint in the Virginia House of Delegates.

The first vote taken in that year was in favor of Henry's position and prompted the formation of a committee to determine how a tax would work. Hearing of his opponent's initial success, Thomas Jefferson wrote James Madison in early December of 1784, "What we have to do, I think, is devoutly to pray for his death."[31] James Madison, almost always more restrained than his passionate friend, had already considered a better plan.

Unbeknownst to Jefferson, in late November of 1784 Madison had supported the elevation of Patrick Henry into the Virginia governor's chair, possibly by working to ensure that Henry ran unopposed. With the major roadblock to his bill removed from the legislature, Madison saw a path forward to victory. The public was on his side, he felt, but the other state legislators needed to hear from their constituents directly. Leaving nothing to chance, Madison helped galvanize opposition to Henry's bill by penning an anonymous petition, the "Memorial and Remonstrance Against Religious Assessments." Beginning the piece with a reiteration of his argument in the debate over Article XVI of the Virginia Bill of Rights—that the right to conscience is unalienable, or untouchable, by the state—Madison described the relationship of God, man, and state in the first of the fifteen-point broadside: "Before any man can be considered as a member of a Civil Society, he must be considered as a subject of the Governor of the Universe. . . ."[32] Madison articulated in the "Memorial" based on a Lockean understanding of the social compact, a unique view of the duties and rights of citizens as they pertain to religion and the state.

The duty that man owes his Creator is religion. "This duty," he wrote, "is precedent both in order of time and degree of obligation, to the claims of Civil Society."[33] Religious duty takes priority to the existence of political arrangements. For Madison, this is true because even before human beings enter society or create a government, they exist as creatures of God. As such, they possess certain rights, including "life, liberty, and property," or as Jefferson put it in the Declaration of Independence, "life, liberty, and the pursuit of happiness."[34] Government exists to protect the rights of citizens. On this foundational idea all of the leading minds of early America agreed.

Madison outlined a relationship between civil society and the right of conscience that is unique. He did so by asking people to think about the theory and practice of property rights. Most people take "property" to mean material possessions. More vital, for Madison, is property that is immaterial or intellectual. The most important possession a human being has is his rights. Just "as a man is said to have a right to his property, he may equally be said to have a property in his rights."[35] Conscience, Madison claimed, "is the most sacred of all property. . . ."[36] Like other intellectual forms of property, conscience is opinion. To be convinced of something, Madison held, following Locke's lead, one must be convinced voluntarily. No one can force you to believe something if you do not freely assent to it. A person might lose her material property to forfeiture, but there is no way for her to lose—or be alienated—from her opinions, including her religious opinions. Conscience resists alienation, or separation from the person because it is theoretically prior to the creation of civil society. Conscience should not be trammeled by the state. On the contrary, if it is doing its job, the state will make the right to conscience inviolate and untouchable.

Madison's practical argument in the "Memorial" built upon this theoretical framework. Religion's integrity, he argued, must not be destroyed by the "arrogant pretension" of the state to control it.[37] Religion is too important to trust to the state, as religion will be damaged in the process. If Virginia's establishment was bolstered, Christianity would become as anemic there as it was everywhere else where it was the official religion. Christians, Madison thus claimed, should be the foremost opponents of establishment; they have the most to lose. What is more, by their own doctrinal lights Christians should see that religious coercion runs contrary to the teaching of the gospel. In economic terms, continued establishment will drive dissenters out of the state and deter newcomers from coming in.

The institutional separation of church and state does not mean that religion has nothing to do with politics. Rather, it means that religion is too vital to entrust to the incompetency of the state. Madison's "Memorial" amounts to an appeal for the adoption of three types of humility:

1. intellectual humility that says truth does not need the backing of the state to win;
2. religious humility that says people cannot be coerced into salvation; and

3. political humility that says the sovereign cannot repeal conscience, so it should not try to do so.

The combination of astute scholarship and sharp politicking that characterized Madison's entire legislative career was on full display in his drafting and circulation of the "Memorial." Intent upon winning over his fellow citizens without unfairly attacking his opponents, Madison blended the art of rhetoric with the knowledge of where his fellow citizens stood on the issue. How might they be moved, he asked, by persuasion, not vitriol?

Madison and his allies did not always take the high road in their political skirmishes, but the "Memorial" is an example where high ideas met civic-minded motives. It was also a model of how to build a political coalition, for in forging, early in his career, an alliance between religious dissenters, free thinkers, and others disaffected with the Anglican establishment, Madison made political friends for life. The support of John Leland, a Baptist minister Madison first befriended in the struggle for religious liberty, later yielded what was likely the decisive margin of victory in Madison's bid to represent Orange County at the Virginia ratification convention for the proposed federal Constitution, almost exactly two years after the "Memorial" was circulated.

Madison's work paid off in the short run as well. As petitions signed by the thousands against Henry's bill landed on legislators' desks, it became clear that not only would Henry's bill be defeated but that there was an opportunity for Jefferson's old bill to be revived. The opponents of the bill sought to delay final action on it, hoping that the legislative term would end, but Madison succeeded in pushing it through to final passage just in time. Jefferson's hand had authored the bill, but Madison's legwork made it law. As Jefferson later testified in his *Autobiography*, final victory came only because of "the unwearied exertions of Mr. Madison, in opposition to the endless quibbles, chicaneries, perversions, vexations and delays of lawyers and demi-lawyers."[38] At the time it passed, a weary Madison allowed himself one well-deserved boast. In relating to Jefferson how Bill No. 82 became law, Madison wrote that its final adoption had "in this country extinguished for ever the ambitious hope of making laws for the human mind."[39]

Madison's labor on behalf of the "Memorial" proved that work behind the scenes does not have to mean second best. Very few people at the time he wrote it knew that Madison was the author of the "Memorial." Unlike legislative triumphs today, there was no celebratory bill-signing ceremony at the end of the process, with Madison laying claim to the commemorative pen. In standing up for the rights of Virginia's religious minorities, Madison embodied meekness, which counsels regard for people who are oppressed. Meekness at its best is not weakness, timidity, or indecision. Madison's vigor in Virginia's battle for religious liberty was undeniable. The man who was hard to hear in an assembly hall rose up on behalf of those with no voice. John Marshall, who was on the losing side of the Virginia debate (but on the majority in all but eight Supreme Court decisions in his thirty-four-year tenure), said of Madison that if eloquence is "persuasion by convincing, Mr. Madison was the most eloquent man I ever heard."[40]

"A LUMINOUS AND DISCRIMINATING MIND"

Madison's first task related to the Convention in 1787 was to convince George Washington to participate in it. It was the junior Virginian, then thirty-six years of age, who had to persuade the great general, who was fifty-one, that his nation needed his service once again. Madison's message to Washington, conveyed in frequent correspondence and in a number of visits to Mount Vernon, was that the governing framework of the American states had failed. The Articles of Confederation had been in place as the new nation's constitution for six years, and the states were no more united than they were at its adoption in 1781. Under the Articles, the states were expected to work together in a "firm league of friendship."[41] In reality, each state operated as its own sovereign, and the national government was empowered to do nothing of significance. Congress lacked the power to tax, and there was no independent executive. Because there were so many parties to treaties, the treaties were violated. States trespassed on the rights of other states, and there was no effective means of deciding commercial disputes. Unless the enfeebled Articles were replaced, representative government would be impossible. These were the conclusions Madison outlined in an April 1787 paper, "Vices of the Political System of the United States."[42]

George Washington, the main audience for Madison's handiwork, was so impressed by the argument in "Vices" that he took careful notes on it. He also copied out by hand another report by Madison, "Notes on Ancient and Modern Confederacies," a historical survey that crystallized the inadequacy of the Articles. The junior Virginian's thorough spadework in the theoretical and historical investigations further eroded Washington's own waning confidence in the Articles. As Washington wrote, "We have probably had too good an opinion of human nature in forming our confederation.... We must take human nature as we find it. Perfection falls not to the share of mortals."[43] In sending to his friends and colleagues a possible roster of the Virginia delegation to Philadelphia, Madison included Washington on the list, hoping to build a groundswell of support for the general's attendance. The gambit worked, and after nearly a year of maneuvering by Madison, in late March 1787, Washington signaled his intention to attend the May Philadelphia meeting. The door to future public service that he had left ajar in his 1783 speech upon resigning his generalship was shoved wide open.

Once the Philadelphia Convention was under way, most everything went smoothly for Madison in the first several weeks. The "Virginia Plan" of government, proposed at the outset of the Convention by Edmund Randolph, one of the state's leading figures, owed its boldness to Madison's pre-Convention labors. In calling for a wholly new frame of government, not just a revision to the Articles of Confederation, the Virginia Plan immediately shifted the scope of the Convention and gave Madison the early upper hand in the most contentious subject of the early debate. Small states like Delaware and New Jersey were in favor of a fixed number of representatives for each state in the legislative branch. Larger states advocated proportional representation, which would result in their securing a great number of representatives in Congress. Madison's plan called for a bicameral or two-chambered Congress, in which the number and allocation of members would be based upon population proportionality. Congress, he argued, should have plenary power to legislate where the states are "incompetent" and should be able to exercise a veto over state laws that were incompatible with "the articles of Union."[44] Both the national executive (who would serve a single term) and members of the judiciary were to be selected by the legislative branch.

The final framework of the Constitution had three branches of government, of course, but in little else did it bear resemblance to Madison's early proposal. Rebuffed in his efforts to secure proportionality in both chambers of Congress, Madison was most morose at the end of the Convention about losing the national "negative," or veto, of illegitimate state acts. Historian Forrest McDonald notes that of the seventy-one occasions (most of them up-or-down votes) where Madison's position during the debates was unequivocal, he was on the losing side nearly 60 percent of the time.[45] When ideas he considered critical were rejected by the other members of the Convention, Madison felt a certain sting. But he carried on, avoiding the temptation to publicly denounce his colleagues or privately slander them. Engaging and artful in his argumentation, Madison demonstrated a respect for the work at hand—and for the colleagues with whom he worked—that, despite the slow pace of overall progress that summer, won him the admiration of many in that hot, un-air-conditioned room.

Striking the right balance between adherence to one's own principles and a willingness to adopt others' ideas is the measure of a good statesman. This quality of judgment takes refinement. At the Philadelphia Convention, Madison, at thirty-six, was eight years younger than the average age of the fifty-five delegates who served. For his age, Madison's quality of judgment was off the charts. But

it was certainly not perfect, even by his own admission. He sometimes pressed in on a subject when stepping back might be the better
course of action. In the late eighteenth century, there was no talk of
IQ or emotional intelligence. What Madison had, and what everyone around him could see that he had, was political intelligence.
Thomas Jefferson, his friend and colleague of fifty years, wrote that
Madison possessed a "luminous and discriminating mind."[46]

Madison combined judgment with an indefatigable commitment to work. In addition to framing the entire debate, Madison
made his mark at the Convention in his own arguments (he would
speak on some 150 occasions, third most of any of the delegates),
and in his record of all of the arguments. Keeping a shorthand
record during the deliberations, Madison would flesh out each day's
debates upon the adjournment of official business. He did not serve
as the appointed secretary, but his notes were far superior to the official record. Tweaking them for the sake of accuracy long after the
Convention was done, Madison directed his estate to publish the
notes only after the last delegate had died.

If at the top of America's constitutional edifice are the soaring
towers, beautiful and majestic, of equality and liberty, we can see in
the rest of its architecture a foundation of natural rights and a frame
made up of the separation of legislative, executive, and judicial
powers. Federalism is like a system of flying buttresses—attractive
in its own right but also functional. The architect of America's
Constitution was James Madison, even if all of the details were
not of his design. As to whether he earned the title "Father of the
Constitution," Madison wrote that it was "not the offspring of a single
brain," but the "work of many heads and many hands."[47] Madison's

contention of shared contributions among many is true, but without the framework he provided in his argument for the extended republic, the Constitution likely would not have risen to the heights it has.

Once the Constitution was signed, the battle for ratification ensued. Madison joined in the fray, helping Alexander Hamilton and John Jay in New York by writing twenty-nine of the eighty-five *Federalist* essays. Published in New York newspapers between late November 1787 and March 1788, Madison's essays—what today we would call op-eds—redressed Anti-Federalist claims that the Constitution would install too powerful a national government. Taking his bearings from human nature, as always, Madison wed theory and practice in explicating, sometimes clause by clause, the Constitution's main features. He wrote at a furious pace, producing the equivalent of one editorial by today's standard, every day, for more than three months.

"HOLY ZEAL"

Nine states were needed to put the Constitution into effect. Even had it not looked as though Virginia might be the ninth, Madison would have stood for election to serve at Virginia's ratification convention. George Washington wanted him there, and Madison, as one of the foremost advocates of convention ratification (as opposed to state legislative ratification, which according to Madison would not have had the same force for popular opinion), felt duty bound to seek the seat he ended up winning.

Madison took an active role at the Virginia Convention. At one point in the heated debate (Patrick Henry was his main opponent again and spoke during two-thirds of the recorded debate), Madison asked, "Is there no virtue among us? If there be not, we are in a wretched situation. No theoretical checks—no form of government can render us secure. To suppose that any form of government will secure liberty or happiness without any virtue in the people, is a chimerical idea."[48] Madison's political career was spent destroying chimeras. He advanced a realistic view of human beings because he started with our lived experience and formed his political thought accordingly. Ideologues do the opposite; they start with theory and impose it on reality. The ideologue lives, as Madison wrote in the *Federalist*, as if he could make the Constitution perfect if only it was created "in his closet or in his imagination."[49]

Recognizing that the Constitution was imperfect, Madison had insisted upon its amendability but also wanted a high bar so that it could not be changed whimsically. He reversed his earlier opposition to the Bill of Rights (it would be but a "parchment barrier," repeating rights the people already possessed) so as to ensure that the Constitution would gain ratification. As a representative from Virginia in the first U.S. Congress, Madison was the prime mover of Congress's adoption of the Bill of Rights in 1791. This effort, like so many of his other labors, was tedious and time-consuming. To arrive at the list of amendments that would be taken up by Congress, Madison sifted through 210 possible amendments to the Constitution as had been proposed by the states. Narrowing that number to eighty and then nineteen (whose language would be interwoven throughout the text of the Constitution), the House Committee of the Whole shortened the tally to seventeen to be added at the end, applicable to all the states. The Senate reversed this idea of incorporation—or making the guarantees of rights apply against the states as well as the national government—and consolidated the seventeen into twelve. What is now the First Amendment was in the final congressional vote the third. The first one was dropped, the second was too (but adopted, more than two hundred years later, as the Twenty-Seventh Amendment), and the third through twelfth became known as the Bill of Rights, appended at the end of the Constitution's main text. "Congress shall make no law," the First Amendment begins, "respecting an establishment of religion, or prohibiting the free exercise thereof."[50]

Madison's genius shone brightest in the legislative chamber; in the seat of the executive, especially as president, his work was hesitant, and his decisions sometimes dilatory. His actions against slavery, whose danger he foresaw and whose existence he hated, could have been more concerted. His dealings in politics were not pristine. Madison did not mind operating behind the scenes; in fact, he rather liked it. The politics of legislative action allows this in a way that being secretary of state or president does not. He did much of his major writing without attribution, writing anonymously or pseudonymously the "Memorial and Remonstrance Against Religious Assessments," publishing his twenty-nine *Federalist* essays as Publius, and not taking credit for the famous 1798 "Virginia Resolution" in favor of the robust powers of states. In addition to this work, Madison wrote numerous speeches, statements, and letters for President George Washington during the first term that office existed.

Madison's fruitful collaboration with Washington ended before the first president's death. It dissolved because of differences over policy and party. Madison and Jefferson on one side, and Hamilton on the other, invented the first parties despite their warnings against them, and Washington could not forgive some of the boisterousness the debate took on late in his first term. Madison's opposition to the Jay Treaty, which in 1796 solidified the young nation's trading relationship with Great Britain, marked the last time Madison and Washington would interact meaningfully. Still, upon Washington's death three years later, Madison mourned for the great man and paid him tribute.

In his political theory, Madison emphasized the fallibility of mortal projects. Yet in practice he never stopped trying to improve the chances that the American experiment in self-government would succeed. The Constitution he helped create imposed limits on power, yet it was not weak. The Constitution had to be powerful, in fact, to protect the rights of the people—to let the government do the things it must, so that civil society might flourish. Weak government is as bad as no government, as liberty is lost either way. Ideological efforts that suppose the nature of man can be changed are doomed to fail. The enduring principles embodied in the Constitution must command our "holy zeal," Madison wrote.[51] Reverence for the rule of law is the duty of every American. In 1836, at the age of eighty-five, James Madison died. The first traveling delegate to arrive in Philadelphia for the Constitutional Convention, he was the last of its signers to leave this world.

SIX

ABIGAIL ADAMS

I n early America's "republic of letters," Abigail Adams was among the most energetic and incisive correspondents. Author of more than 2,100 surviving letters, Abigail penned more than half of those to John Adams, her husband of fifty-four years. These letters reveal the thoughts and sentiments of a wife, mother, farmer, and businesswoman who was also a spirited behind-the-scenes stateswoman. Abigail and John wrote to each other a great deal about politics, with her opinions offering deep insight into the leading individuals and events of the day. "Modesty," she wrote of George Washington upon first meeting the general in 1775, "marks every line and feature of his face."[1] After nearly a quarter century of interaction with Washington, Abigail's opinion of his modesty had not changed. Washington, she recollected upon his death, never let the "adulation" that accompanied him during his life make him "forget that he was a man, subject to the weakness and frailty attached to human nature."[2] The first president was "wise," she affirmed, while the fourth, James Madison, was learned.

Abigail was known as learned and often wise, but her husband, John, was rarely mistaken for being modest or humble. Madison, for one, so resented the "extravagant self-importance" of John Adams, as he described it to Thomas Jefferson, that he never saw fit to have a private meeting with him.[3] As one of John's contemporaries said, he "wants magnanimity."[4] When lacking, neither magnanimity nor humility is easily obtained.

"A PERFECT CANDOR"

Not long before they were to be married, twenty-nine-year-old John Adams wrote his nineteen-year-old fiancée, Abigail Smith, about the balance he hoped she would impart to him:

> But you who have always softened and warmed my heart, shall restore my benevolence as well as my health and tranquility of mind. You shall polish and refine my sentiments of life and manners, banish all the unsocial and ill natured particles in my composition, and form me to that happy temper that can reconcile a quick discernment with a perfect candor.[5]

Partly the effusions of a literary-minded young man who had fallen lovestruck for a splendid young woman, John's statement was also a sincerely expressed hope for the possibility of a mate who would smooth his wrinkles. It was followed by a ferocious critique of one of Abigail's male friends.

The daughter of a Congregationalist minister, Abigail was faithful not only in her religious convictions but also in her fidelity to friends. In response to his harsh words about her friend, Abigail implored John to temper such judgments and recover his "former tranquility of mind."[6] What's more, she seemed somewhat alarmed that John thought that *her* virtue could stand in for *his* vices. Abigail observed such a sharp tongue in him that she believed that people clammed up in his presence. When John wrote expressing his confidence in her ability to be good on account of both of them, it is little wonder, then, that Abigail was concerned. As historian Woody Holton notes, "Breaking off their wedding engagement was the furthest thing from her mind" after she received that letter. Still, she "could not help wondering anew whether she would really be happy spending the rest of her life with a man who could be so arrogant and cruel."[7]

Early on, when John thought Abigail could be an antidote against his own arrogance, while John and Abigail were yet courting, a smallpox epidemic raged through the American colonies. When Abigail's uncle and the family's physician, Cotton Tufts, urged John to take the smallpox inoculation, the young man at first resisted and then agreed to it. Abigail herself wanted to receive the pox from her uncle, but her parents would not assent. Upon hearing that John would undergo the procedure, Abigail wrote Dr. Tufts to tell him how pleased she was that her beloved would "submit." His stubborn pride usually won out, but in this case he had listened to others, and to her. Shortly before her uncle received John, Abigail wrote to ask the doctor's encouragement of such submission by her beau, so that in the future he "will in many cases follow it."[8] Tufts served Abigail (and John) well for many years thereafter as a financial trustee and adviser.

Contrary to Thomas Jefferson's claim about John Adams that he was not only vain but also blind to it, John had long demonstrated at least a private acknowledgment of his problem with pride.[9] As early as 1756, just after his graduation from Harvard College, John had confessed to his diary,

> Oh! That I could wear out of my mind every mean and base affectation; conquer my natural pride and self-conceit, expect no more deference from my fellows than I deserve, acquire that meekness and humility which are the sure mark and characters of a great and generous soul, and subdue every unworthy passion. . . . How happy should I then be in the favor and good will of all honest men and the sure prospect of a happy immortality![10]

Despite his early awareness of his problem, John's struggle did not get any easier with time. In May 1789, just after Adams had been installed as America's first vice president, a visiting Frenchman wrote to his brother attempting to capture the distance between the fulsome praise given Adams in America and the reality of his character: "These trite and exaggerated flatteries must be quite disagreeable to a man who is portrayed as the most austere, humble, and simple republican; but it seems that he does not dislike it as much as it is said he does; and under the philosophical cloak, a tiny bit of ear is showing."[11] Everyone cares about what is said of them by other people, but for Adams there seemed more than a tiny bit of ear showing. After Adams had served his single term as second president of the United States, the Englishman Thomas Paine wrote about him, "It has been the political career of this man to begin with hypocrisy, proceed with arrogance, and finish in contempt." All "such characters" deserved this "fate," Paine concluded, less than charitably.[12]

John and Abigail were married in 1764. Throughout their more than half a century of marriage, Abigail propped John up on the side to which he leaned. Her humility could never fully counterbalance his excess pride, for neither marriage nor life works that way, but in ways small and large Abigail helped her husband. Abigail was an honest soul and a modest one too. Often associated with one's outward appearance, modesty is in reality much more about an interior disposition. Like humility, it is tied to truthfulness about one's own soul. It demands honesty about things invisible. Contrary to popular misconceptions, modesty is not the underestimation of one's worth. Rather, it acts as a restraint against the inordinate desire for recognition. While everyone desires recognition, a modest person quells the longing for fleeting fame. Modesty checks the impulse to claim credit and crave praise. It is the anti-vanity. "Praise is a dangerous sweet," Abigail warned her son Charles when he was eleven years old, "unless properly tempered. If it does not make you arrogant, assuming and self sufficient, but on the contrary fires your breast with emulation to become still more worthy and engaging," it can be worthwhile. "But if you ever feel your little bosom swell with pride and begin to think yourself better than others; you will then become less worthy, and lose those qualities which now make you valuable."[13]

What Abby and John sought to teach their children was that

success in life requires the careful cultivation of virtue, and the surest foundation of virtue is religion. Living with consistent adherence to virtue in public and private is the mark of a good human being and citizen. For the virtue of humility, gaining consistency between the public and private realms is of special challenge, for humility can be false and convincing in public and utterly absent in private. As John wrote to their longtime friend, "The longer I live and the more I see of public men, the more I wish to be a private one. Modesty is a virtue that can never thrive in public. Modest merit! Is there such a thing remaining in public life?"[14] How is it possible, John asked, when the public man is puffing himself up, to not stay puffed up in private? Neither he nor Abby had the perfect answer to this question, but their life together marked an impressive attempt at answering it.

"YOU SHINE AS A STATESWOMAN"

As a woman in Massachusetts, Abigail was not allowed to vote or otherwise have much of a voice in the public square. This deprivation did not mean that the public-spirited and pugnacious Abigail shied away from following the events of the day; in fact, she frequently weighed in on them with friends and family, especially John. In the early 1770s, when the American colonists were trying to decide whether to throw off the British, John's star began rising in Massachusetts and throughout New England. As the issues to which John, an attorney and political thinker, dedicated himself became more prominent—taxation, representation, the form of governments—John's notoriety did too. His writings urging

"independency" were little sparks. As Abigail said of the movement as a whole, in 1773, "The flame is kindled and like lightning it
catches from soul to soul."[15]

One pamphlet, published in January 1776, fanned the flames of
revolutionary zeal more than any other. It was not written by John
Adams, who was working on his own treatise (later published as
"Thoughts on Government"), but rather by the Englishman Thomas
Paine. "Common Sense" was printed more than 150,000 times,
which in a nation of three million people meant that nearly everyone knew its argument, even if they did not own a copy. Most, like
Abigail, loved Paine's attack on the monarchy. Only a few, like John,
deplored its "democratical" spirit, which lacked "any restraint or even
an attempt at any equilibrium or counterpoise."[16] Abigail shared that
criticism of Paine's work, but that did not preclude her from praising
it unstintingly and recommending it widely. Nor did she stop singing
its praises even though John was clearly upset that Paine's attack on
the Crown, and not his own work, had electrified the nation. Abigail's
refusal to soothe her husband's hurt ego might have been an effort to
tamp down his pride and make him more prudent in the process. Envy
born of arrogance can cripple a statesman, and Abigail did not want
it to undo her husband. Even more, she cared a great deal about her
country and put it above the protection of John's ego.

Abigail Adams was humble in her service to her family, her husband, her fellow citizens, and her country. She was obedient to her
duty, but she acted out of strength, not servility. Hers was a private
sacrifice on behalf of the public good. She sought recognition for
herself, for women as a whole, and for her husband, but her seeking
was moderated by a higher good than any of those—the common

good. In ably taking on the tasks required to maintain the Adams's family farm in Braintree, Massachusetts, nearly fifteen miles outside of Boston, Abigail enabled John to have the time to focus on public service. For ten out of their first twenty years of marriage, Abigail and John were apart. A deep love between the two, and for the cause of liberty, kept them united in spirit despite their physical separation.

Abigail relished political things and sponged all she could from John about his work on behalf of the Revolutionary cause, and then later, in building a constitutional foundation both for the Commonwealth of Massachusetts and the country. An astute observer of both the battlefield and backroom deals, Abigail was her husband's closest confidante, always ready with a word of advice, even when it contradicted his own conclusions. Her contributions to the success of the family were not the stuff of headlines; nonetheless, they spoke loudly to all who were around John and Abigail. As patriot Fisher Ames wrote his fellow New Yorker Rufus King, "She is as complete a politician as any lady in the old French court."[17] Others saw her outstanding abilities as well. In September 1775, after a visiting Englishman had called Abigail "the most accomplished lady he had seen since he left England," John wrote to his wife, "You see a Quaker can flatter, but don't you be proud."[18] Coming some eleven years into their marriage, and from a man who even at this early stage in his career was almost legendarily vain, this cheeky rebuke was ignored by Abigail. It was John who needed the warning, as he himself confessed to his diary, "Down, vanity, for you don't know who this Englishman is."[19]

The personal and political come together in Abigail's life in the Greek idea of *oikonomia*, or the prudent management of the household. Mastering the family affairs in farming, finance, animal husbandry, and child rearing—not to mention the affairs of state— was Abigail's calling. John was proud of his wife. "You shine as a stateswoman, of late as well as a farmeress," he wrote her in 1776.[20]

Throughout her life, Abigail displayed a fierce allegiance to the American way of life. Before independence, she was keen on pressuring Britain through economic means, making do in the Adams household with what could be created in the colonies. During the war, having witnessed the Battle of Bunker Hill firsthand, along with their firstborn son, John Quincy, Abigail later sat on the Committee of Ladies, which was to decide the fate of the left-behind Tory women. After the war, Abigail knew that building a new nation would require the virtuous efforts of not just some but all Americans. In this she embodied the American spirit that would emerge in the 1780s.

Knowing both the disorder of wartime hardship and the burdens of British domination, Abigail became an ardent defender of American constitutionalism. In the way she lived and in what she wrote to John and others, she advanced one of the leading insights of American constitutionalism: for a written constitution to mean anything it had to fit together with the unwritten constitution of the people. Principles and practice had to be bound together. For Abigail, that meant starting with human nature, which is selfish at base. It is not irremediably so, for human beings can elevate their gazes and pursue goals beyond their narrow self-interest. A state like Massachusetts (John wrote its constitution in 1780, and it is still in place) and a country like the United States cannot create constitutions supposing people to be unselfish. That fact, however, does not mean that citizens should quit working to advance the common good. Rather, human nature means that those efforts must be redoubled. Advancing the common good can be done in grand ways, like her husband did in the halls of Congress and in the diplomatic parlor rooms of England, France, and the Netherlands. It can also be done as Abigail did, in the steady support of her family, friends, church, and local community. The unwritten constitution is woven in that work, later to be knit together with the written document. Only when the unwritten and written constitutions come together is our liberty made whole.

"TOO BIG FOR THE HOUSE"

Abigail knew that her husband's work was important, but that knowledge did little to lessen the pain she felt at his frequent absences from home. In their courtship and early in their marriage, the absences were shorter and the tone of their letters often lighter. In John's February 14, 1763, missive to Abigail, written before they were married, he looks forward to seeing her on the Sabbath: "I mount this moment for that noisy, dirty town of Boston, where Parade, Pomp, Nonsense Frippery, Folly, Foppery, Luxury, Politics, and the soul-Confounding Wrangles of the Law will give me the higher relish for Spirit, Taste and Sense, at Weymouth, next Sunday."[21] On another occasion, after they had been married but a short time, Abigail expressed her loneliness: "Alas! How many snow banks divide thee and me and my warmest wishes to see thee will not melt one of them."[22]

Later, when the absences grew longer, many of Abigail's letters to

John read as if they were stained with tears. During the Revolution, when the press of duty for John sometimes meant that levity was replaced with what could sound to Abigail like lectures or perfunctory business reports, her complaints were sharp. As she wrote John in 1775,

> All the letters I receive from you seem to be written in so much haste that they scarcely leave room for a social feeling. They let me know that you exist, but some of them contain scarcely six lines. I want some sentimental effusions of the heart. I am sure you are not destitute of them. Or are they all absorbed in the great public? Much is due to that, I know, but, being part of the public, I lay claim to a larger share than I have had.[23]

In between these early absences, when John was becoming one of the most highly regarded attorneys in the land, and later, when he was the commander in chief of the new country, John served as an ambassador, seeking the peace as well as commercial agreements between the United States and Holland, France, and Great Britain. These overseas absences were among the most painful for both John and Abigail. All three of their sons were at various points able to accompany their father overseas, but this did nothing to mitigate the pain of their parents' separation. They could endure it only because of their shared recognition that such sacrifice on behalf of their country was worth it.

Late in 1783, with John having implored Abigail to make her way to him in The Hague, Netherlands, Abigail responded, reflecting upon how difficult it would be for her to go and how impossible it would be for her to stay. More than the danger of an ocean crossing caused her concern. "But a mere American as I am, unacquainted with the etiquette of the courts, taught to say the thing I mean, and to wear my heart in my countenance, I am sure I should make an awkward figure." Lacking any formal education, Abigail wondered also about her social skills. "And then it would mortify my pride," she wrote John, "if I should be thought to disgrace you." Yet despite this worry, Abigail displayed a confidence born of her American spirit-edness: "Yet strip royalty of its pomp, and power, and what are its votaries more than their fellow worms?"[24]

Abigail was a republican through and through and also a Puritan. Her husband might have become an ambassador, feted by kings and queens and nobles, but their family's lifestyle in Massachusetts remained the same as it was when, early in his diplomatic career, his efforts to gain audience with almost anyone overseas were rebuffed. Responding to townsfolk who wondered why the Adamses did not change their mode of living commensurate with John's climb into the top echelon of global politics, Abigail related a tale she had come across about a minister in Queen Elizabeth's court. As biographer Edith Gelles relates the story, "When the queen visited him, she remarked about his modest home. He responded: 'The house, may it please your Majesty, is big enough for the man, but you have made the man too big for the house.'"[25] As Abigail later related, "I have so little of the ape about me that I have refused every public invitation . . . and sequestered myself in this humble cottage, content with rural life and my domestic employments in the midst of which I have sometimes smiled, upon recollecting that I had the honor of being allied to an ambassador."[26]

In mid-1784, Abigail set sail for England, from there to travel to

Paris. Traveling along with her oldest daughter, also named Abigail but known as Nabby, Mrs. Adams would stay united with John for the next four years (and with her daughter and two of her sons for much of that time). Elated to be with her husband and family, Abigail never gained a high comfort level in France or England, as she had nothing of the courtier spirit in her. She found their experience among the French royalty and courtesans especially troublesome.

Later, after she had returned to Massachusetts and John had returned to London, Abigail reflected upon the pain of yet another absence by him. Calling her country "hard-hearted," Abigail wrote, "No man even if he is sixty years of age ought to have more than three months at a time from his family." She continued, "It has committed more robberies upon me, and obliged me to more sacrifices than any other woman in the country and this I will maintain against anyone who will venture to come forward and dispute it with me. As there never can be a compensation for me, I must sit down with this consolation that it might have been worse."[27]

When Abigail later rose with John to the height of American prestige upon his election as second president of the United States of America in 1796, she shouldered her duties with aplomb—and dread. When she was in Philadelphia, she pulled off her social responsibilities very ably but did not relish that part of her job. Lacking experience in formal social settings, Abigail did the best she could when meeting and greeting the glitterati of the day. She was much more at home on the farm, or even better, bandying political advice about with John. Abigail worried that even without a permanent relocation to Philadelphia, her new life (which in reality was not all that glamorous) would lead her to vanity and excess pride in other forms. To her friends and family she wrote an appeal that in their correspondence and in their other interactions they would keep her accountable—and honest.[28]

"REMEMBER THE LADIES"

When Abigail wrote of her humble role at home, it was not an empty boast. She could have been a social climber, and had she heeded the urgings of her husband, she might have abandoned their farm and hired out all of its maintenance much earlier. She had help in her domestic duties, but in opting to stay on the farm (even when John was president, she spent a total of only eighteen months with him in Philadelphia, and then later, in Washington, D.C.), she preserved the family's main source of income without reliance upon a single slave. Always caring for the infirm in her immediate and extended family, Abigail endured the sadness of losing two children, including a stillborn daughter and another girl, Susanna, who failed to reach her second birthday. Her son Charles never pulled himself together, nor did the man Nabby ended up marrying. Sadness was her constant companion, yet Abigail's indomitable spirit inspired the family to press on.

All of these duties might have rendered a weaker person incapable of action outside of her personal sphere. Yet politics was a constant preoccupation of Abigail, and her letters abound with excitement about military matters (she would update her husband regularly about the Revolutionary War progress), domestic intrigue (Abigail maintained a love-hate relationship with Thomas Jefferson that mirrored that of her husband's), and plain old political gossip. When John was abroad and Abigail had not yet joined him, she was his chief correspondent for domestic affairs. When both were stateside, Abigail kept him in the loop with whatever she could glean from the newspapers, as well as the newsmakers who would regularly visit her. She demanded the same from John and could be grouchy when he failed to keep her updated. Despite the domestic sphere allotted the female sex, women "inherit an equal share of curiosity," Abigail insisted.[29] Hers was never sated, and despite John's occasional grumpiness and sometimes taciturn correspondence, he prized the sage advice of his wife.

He saw in his "dearest friend" a partner in everything he did, including the sacred duty of public service. In the same letter in which John wrote Abigail, "Liberty once lost is lost forever,"[30] he praised her fortitude: "You are really brave, my dear, you are a heroine."[31] Signing her letters during the American Revolution as Portia, after the wife of Brutus, Caesar's assassin, Abigail signaled an admiration not for the Roman woman's suicide but instead her sacrifice on behalf of the republic. In taking that pen name with a few correspondents, including John, Abigail indicated her own strong sense of duty to the Revolutionary cause. She joked about taking on another name too during the war. To Elizabeth Welles Adams, the wife of patriot Sam Adams, John's second cousin, Abigail wrote that they were "sister delegates." As wives of congressmen (both men were serving in the Continental Congress), after all, Abigail put her question to John and Sam, "Why should we not assume your titles when we give you up our names?"[32]

Mindful of America's commitment to equality, Abigail was

curious throughout her adult life to know what this commitment could mean for women. Patriarchy, she knew firsthand and in her study of history, was an unjust system down to its roots. While working for its end in America was not yet feasible, Abigail nonetheless sought to chop off its most rotten limbs. The deprivation of private property rights to married women, for example, within the Anglo-American tradition of law, was the immediate cause that impelled Abigail to pen the words for which she is so famous—"Remember the ladies."[33] The broader context of her discussion with John on the subject was slavery, which Abigail and John had always firmly opposed. "I have sometimes been ready to think," Abigail ventured, "that the passion for liberty cannot be equally strong in the breasts of those who have been accustomed to deprive their fellow creatures of theirs." Speaking specifically of Virginians but concerned about any American who owned slaves, Abigail was "certain" that slavery "is not founded upon that generous and Christian principle of doing to others as we would that others should do unto us."[34] Slavery was a great evil—a sin, in fact—and its continuation in the colonies was a stain upon the land.

Many years later, when the Adamses were in Philadelphia, Abigail had occasion to repeat the golden rule in defense of equal rights. As biographer David McCullough relates the story, James Prince, a freeman taught by Abigail how to read and write, was eager to join a new school for apprentices. Upon her encouragement he enrolled, but his attendance was quickly challenged by one of Abigail's neighbors, who threatened that unless Prince withdrew, the school would empty of other pupils and cease operations. "The boy is a freeman as much as any of the young men, and merely because his face is black is he to be denied instruction?" Abigail asked the neighbor, citing the golden rule. "Tell them," she wrote of the other boys at the school, "that I hope we shall all go to Heaven together."[35] The school stayed open, and James Prince stayed a student there.

By the same rationale that guided her opposition to slavery, Abigail wished for greater equality between men and women in America. Women should be accorded property rights so that within the sacred bonds of marriage they, like their British counterparts, might enjoy the individual right of private property. Abigail's serious plea was met with a playful jest by her husband: Who knew, he wrote, with reference to Indian uprisings in America, that there was "another tribe more numerous and powerful than the rest" that had "grown discontented?"[36] He then offered the idea, none too pleasing to Abigail, that women always have had the real power in marriage. She need not worry, he wrote, offering a kind of pat on her head from afar. She did not much appreciate the puppy dog treatment. "I cannot say that I think you very generous to the ladies," she volleyed in her next letter, "for whilst you are proclaiming peace and good will to men, emancipating all nations, you insist upon retaining an absolute power over wives. But you must remember that arbitrary power is like most other things which are very hard, very liable to be broken."[37]

In denouncing tyranny, Abigail had in mind both the enslavement of Africans on the soil of the United States and the deprivation of rights that were owed to women. Abigail's larger point in decrying slavery and in challenging John and his fellow patriots to stand up for women's property rights was one of concern for the disadvantaged, a cause she maintained with consistency throughout her life. Whether in her personal care for family, friends, and neighbors enduring hardship, or her broader social and political concerns, Abigail urged action to remedy clear cases of injustice. She not only urged action but acted herself with a prudent regard for what was possible and right. She was firm in advocacy of liberty under law and of justice for all. She also acted with wit and a little whimsy, for while she might have recoiled at John's rebuff of her appeal on behalf of "the ladies," she did not respond with overheated rhetoric. Instead, she took action in the areas in which she could.

Education was a preoccupation of Abigail Adams. Aware of and even embarrassed about her own lack of a liberal education, Abigail became an ardent autodidact, devouring everything she could in John's library. After John introduced her to Mercy Otis Warren, wife of Revolutionary War veteran Colonel James Warren and sister of patriot James Otis Jr., Abigail asked her new well-educated friend to advance her own education. As Edith Gelles relates, in following up on their first in-person meeting, Abigail had to overcome a fear that compared to the formidable Warren, she would prove an inadequate interlocutor. Worried that she would not be up to the high standards of Warren's learning, Abigail expressed her hope that nonetheless the more senior woman might take Abigail under her wing. "Though like the timorous bird," Abigail might "fail in the attempt and tumble to the ground," she wanted Warren to know that it would never be for lack of "effort." Speaking of their recent stay at the Warren home, she continued, "nor will I suffer my pride, (which is greatly increased since my more intimate acquaintance with you) to debar me the pleasure" of taking up the correspondence.[38] As Gelles writes about this appeal from a woman of little education to another of much erudition, "Abigail's letter exudes humility, not just out of proper literary convention, but because of her sincere awe for the learning as well as the social stature of her new acquaintance."[39] The friendship that resulted between the two women, documented in a rich exchange of letters, brought a lifetime of rewards for both them and their families.

Abigail's awareness of her own lack of formal education made her resolve that Nabby would not be so deprived. To John, who wrote to her that "New England must produce the heroes, the statesmen, the philosophers, or America will make no great figure for some time,"[40] Abigail shot back, "If we mean to have heroes, statesmen and philosophers, we should have learned women."[41] With Nabby, Abigail acted on this resolution, giving her daughter an education in the classics, including Greek and Latin, unusual for the day. John agreed to this pedagogy but asked that they keep it quiet. Abigail's example pushed John to write her—even before her "Remember the ladies" missive—that he wished that women could participate more fully in politics. They should be able to act "upon a larger scale," to uphold "the great principles of virtue and freedom of political regulations," perhaps in the process even saving "whole nations and generations from misery, want and contempt."[42]

When denied direct access to levers of power, Abigail Adams occasionally employed indirection to seize them. Deprived by law of the ability to own property or sign contracts, despite the fact that for much of her married life Abigail served as the family's treasurer, accountant, and real estate agent, she nonetheless had to go through John for the acquisition of any property. Most of the time—because of the splendid partnership she had with her husband—she did so gladly but with annoyance at the general principle of the exclusion. Occasionally, when John and Abigail disagreed about a particular piece of property or an investment opportunity (they were never wealthy but always frugal), Abigail counted on the long-standing trust between her and Cotton Tufts, the family's financial adviser. In one instance, Abigail served advance warning of money that was to be conveyed to him by John Quincy. "With this money which I call mine," she wrote the doctor, instructing him that it was to be deployed to purchase government bonds. As historian Holton notes, that very phrase "money which I call mine" was an unruly sentiment coming from a woman; her actions marked another level of boldness. Tufts complied with her request and set up the transaction to shield Abigail from any later blame.[43]

Abigail admired her husband with complete devotion. She was a fierce defender of him and his public policies—even when she privately disputed them, which was not often. She knew better than anyone else, in fact, his faults and his finest attributes. She knew how much it pained her impatient, even "pushful" John to play second fiddle to George Washington as his vice president and throughout his career. "For myself I have little ambition or pride," Abigail wrote a friend, "for my *Husband* I freely own I have much."[44] Despite the care she took to protect her husband's reputation and the concern she demonstrated for John, Abigail could be neither humble nor modest on his behalf. Nonetheless, her example undoubtedly helped him even as he struggled to keep his pride in check. Abigail was modest about her accomplishments in the face of adversity and humble also about her purposes for striving. Personal and political successes were not ends in themselves but means to the betterment of her family and her country.

"There were times, my friend, in Boston which tried women's souls as well as men's," John wrote to Abigail in 1770. Abigail's life was marked by trying times. It was also marked by her meeting the high challenges placed before her. In a marriage that helped to define America, Abigail undoubtedly raised John's character, even as she helped to do the same for her country. In turn, John honored her and appreciated how she made him a better man. Perhaps with his wife in mind, John offered advice to their daughter Nabby as she contemplated a spouse: "Think of no other greatness but that of the soul, no other riches but those of the heart."[45] Abigail Adams was a magnanimous woman.

SEVEN

ABRAHAM LINCOLN

Just over two weeks after John Adams bid his final farewell to Abigail, upon her death in 1818, nine-year-old Abraham Lincoln lost his mother. Abraham Lincoln was born in a log cabin, and his "humble" roots are well known today. For a good number of Lincoln's contemporaries, however, *humble* was an unlikely adjective to describe the man himself. William Herndon, Lincoln's longtime law partner, did not think Lincoln was humble, nor did John Hay, Lincoln's longtime presidential secretary. So great was his ambition, in fact, that both Herndon and Hay agreed that Lincoln was almost wholly lacking in humility.

Serenely seated as if on a throne, Abraham Lincoln, god-like, looks out over the National Mall in Washington, D.C. To enter Lincoln's temple a pilgrim must climb nearly a hundred stairs and cross a threshold guarded by twelve massive columns. Then, instead of having to walk through a long hall as in temples or courts of old, a visitor to this democratic shrine is met immediately with a nineteen-foot-tall statue. The curiosity, even awe, with which people from across the globe enter the Lincoln Memorial is equaled only by the excitement inside its chamber. Children have to crane their necks to gain a glimpse of Lincoln's face. Above his marble head, there is a short inscription:

IN THIS TEMPLE
AS IN THE HEARTS OF THE PEOPLE
FOR WHOM HE SAVED THE UNION
THE MEMORY OF ABRAHAM LINCOLN
IS ENSHRINED FOREVER.

Abraham Lincoln lives in the hearts of Americans like no other hero. When we travel to his memorial by the millions, it is not to worship the man inside but to remember what he revered—for on the walls of the temple are Lincoln's words calling Americans to tasks neither easy nor outdated. His plea, to Americans of his age and ours alike, was that we live not by his lights but by those that burned in 1776. Lincoln's own words point us not to his person but to undying principles. It is a rare temple that impresses upon people that self-government is the thing most needed, but then again, Lincoln was among the rarest of men.

What made him rare, like George Washington, was his ability to refine raw ambition and in the process impose self-restraint upon his soul. "I claim no extraordinary exemption from personal ambition," Abraham Lincoln said in 1858.[1] His ambition was extraordinary, but his desire for power, influence, and personal prestige, as Lincoln admitted, was common among human beings. His ability to bring order to his soul was born of humility honed not for political gain but for the health of the nation.

"POLITICAL RELIGION"

That Lincoln is memorialized in a temple befits the man who urged Americans to adopt what he called a "political religion." Even before he turned thirty years of age, Abraham Lincoln was worried about America's future. The heroes of 1776, he lamented in an 1838 speech to the Young Men's Lyceum, in Springfield, Illinois, were being lost every day. What "the silent artillery of time has done," he said, was remove from the American people's everyday experience the physical reminder of the courage needed to win the American Revolution—and to keep the republic. The "pillars of the temple of liberty," as he referred to the veterans of the War for Independence, were falling.[2] As a sad consequence of this fact, Americans had to find inspiration elsewhere.

For Abraham Lincoln, the source of the inspiration was of most consequence. Passions stirred up by politicians, Lincoln told his audience of citizens in Springfield, the state capital, would prove unreliable inspiration. Nor could inspiration come from anger like that of a mob. Passions are forms of unruliness, he argued, and anything they inspire will more likely lead to tyranny than liberty. Instead of passion, we need reason, Lincoln insisted. "Reason, cold, calculating, unimpassioned reason, must furnish all the materials for our future support and defense."[3] If we judge Lincoln's speech by this line alone, his advice sounds Machiavellian. "Cold, calculating, unimpassioned" reason? Surely the man who would become the Great Emancipator and the author of the Gettysburg Address could come up with something more inspiring for his audience?

Lincoln urged his audience, and in turn, us today, to be reasonable because he knew that reason enables reverence. Knowledge of principles long ago established should inspire in Americans a reverence for the laws, Lincoln argued. This reverence could not be fleeting, like too many of the emotions inspired by the tent meetings of Lincoln's day—gone as soon as the charismatic preacher left town. This reverence had to be enduring, held aloft not by hot air but cold reason, not a spur-of-the-moment burst of passion but a right reason that knew how and why it arrived at its conclusion.

For Lincoln, like Madison before him, the only reasonable inspiration for future generations to fight for liberty was a reverential regard for the Constitution. He made the case for this reverence in the Lyceum Address, urging "every lover of liberty" to abide by the nation's laws. "As the patriots of seventy-six did to the support of the Declaration of Independence, so to the support of the Constitution and Laws, let every American pledge his life, his property, and his sacred honor." Civic education in the form of "reverence for the laws" must be taught from infancy, Lincoln said, so that as children grew into adults they would adopt it as their "political religion." Encouraging Americans to "sacrifice unceasingly" upon the "altars" of the political religion, Lincoln was quick to note, does not mean that all of the laws of the land are just. If they are not, they must be changed.[4] But they must be changed according to constitutional and legal means, not just tossed out because what Lincoln called a "mobocratic spirit" prevailed.[5]

Lincoln urged religious devotion—reverence—that was reasonable because he knew how dangerous unruly passions can be. They are dangerous not just to the body politic but also to the human soul. Humility helps us govern our passions. The lower parts of the soul must be controlled by the higher, and humility helps to order the passions by restraining the most tyrannical of them. To borrow Lincoln's language from the concluding words of his First Inaugural Address, humility helps us live up to the "better angels of our nature" by reminding us that other forces vie for control of our souls.[6]

As a virtue, humility has an ordering quality to it. Arrogance has the opposite effect, as it loosens the grip of self-control and throws a human soul into disorder. As Lincoln made clear in his Lyceum Address, he was aware of the power of arrogance, especially as it takes the form of unchecked ambition. Ambition is not evil itself, but when an individual lets ambition run wild, it has the tendency to take over his soul. When this happens, a person loses sight of limitations. He is deluded into thinking himself unbeatable. Arrogance gives rise to unchecked ambition and begins a vicious cycle. Unchecked ambition tends to make those in its thrall more and more arrogant. And the arrogant continue to grow in misdirected ambition. This cycle—arrogance feeding ambition, and ambition giving way to more arrogance—can produce a tyrant. How can ambition be channeled, Lincoln asked, to avoid the creation of an American tyrant?

Ambition is like pride in one decisive respect. Held in check, it is immensely important to the accomplishment of high and difficult tasks. Left unchecked, it is a debilitating force. Pride in check can be balanced with humility. One can be properly proud of some accomplishment and at the same time humble. We will see this combination in the life of Frederick Douglass, whose life we will cover next. We also see it in the life of Abraham Lincoln. Ambition, like pride, is kept in check if it is directed to proper ends. Like healthy pride, there is also worthy ambition.

Speaking with admiration about the American Founding Fathers, Abraham Lincoln noted in his Lyceum Address that their ambition was to create a lasting experiment premised upon "the capability of a people to govern themselves." The Founders were ambitious. They even aspired to immortality, Lincoln claimed. They knew they might achieve this fame if they succeeded. "If they failed, they were to be called knaves and fools, and fanatics for a fleeting hour; then to sink and be forgotten."[7] Their experiment was ambitious and risky.

It was also "successful," Lincoln said, so much so that he wondered whether future Americans—ambitious for honor, just as the Founders were—would be satisfied by following in their footsteps. "Towering genius disdains a beaten path," he said. "It seeks regions hitherto unexplored." Having noted the profound problem of a successful founding "experiment" and how that success might make future generations intent upon blazing their own path, Lincoln said of "towering genius" that it "thirsts and burns for distinction; and, if possible, it will have it, whether at the expense of emancipating slaves, or enslaving freemen."[8]

What did Lincoln foresee in the country's future? His vision had to have alarmed some in his audience. "Is it unreasonable then to expect, that some man possessed of the loftiest genius, coupled with ambition sufficient to push it to its utmost stretch, will at some time, spring up among us?" Just to ensure that his point was clear, earlier in his speech Lincoln noted that he was thinking of an Alexander, Julius Caesar, or Napoleon. These men, members of "the family of the lion, or the tribe of the eagle," would never have been satisfied with a typical political job.[9] They yearned for something much greater.

What about Abraham Lincoln? What did he want? Was a young Abe, listening to his heart, becoming aware of ambition on a scale much greater than that satisfied by a seat in Congress? The closing to his Lyceum Address offers no clear answers to these questions, but it does reveal an important insight into the object of Lincoln's reverence. Calling for "general intelligence, sound morality and, in particular, a reverence for the Constitution and the laws," Lincoln ended his speech by paying tribute to George Washington. Until a trumpet awakens "our Washington," Lincoln challenged his fellow citizens that they have a high task: to ensure that they can die knowing "that we revered his name to the last" and that "during his long sleep, we permitted no hostile foot to pass over or desecrate [his] resting place."[10]

Lincoln's peroration may sound like he was setting himself up as the next George Washington. Yet in his rhetoric as a whole, including this speech, Lincoln does not set himself up as the hero or the sole inheritor of the Founders' legacy. Politicians are adept at the practice of situating themselves in a narrative of troubled times so it appears that only they—the indispensable ones—will be able to get the country out of the mess it is in. It would have been easy for Lincoln to lapse into this kind of talk later in life, for in fact he, like Washington, was indispensable to the survival of the republic. The irony of this, of course, is that if either man had started to believe in his indispensability, the republic likely would not have survived.

"A LITTLE ENGINE THAT KNEW NO REST"

Lincoln's law partner in Springfield, William Herndon, famously said of his associate of two decades, "His ambition was a little engine that knew no rest."[11] Even so, Lincoln's little engine had an uphill climb all the way. By the time he delivered the Lyceum Address, Lincoln had little to celebrate in his professional or personal life. Lacking family connections and a formal education, Lincoln had a strong belief in can-do entrepreneurship that was matched with a personal record of failed business ventures, including one unsuccessful retail effort that left him mired in debt.

Lincoln's first foray into politics was no more successful. Introducing himself in his first political speech in Pappsville, Illinois, in March 1832, the young man said, "I presume you all know who I am. I am humble Abraham Lincoln." He went on to say, "My politics are short and sweet, like the old woman's dance."[12] Humble Abe's first dance in politics was short but not sweet. He lost the election for a seat in the state legislature.

Lincoln's early personal fortunes fared no better than those of his entrepreneurial and political affairs. Having landed in Springfield only to fall out of love with his fiancée, Lincoln had the unhappy task of breaking his engagement with Mary Owens. This he did only after he failed in ham-handed efforts to convince her that maybe she was not so fond of him as she imagined. Lawyering, which he entered into in earnest early in 1837, suited his mind and disposition more than any other endeavor he had tried up to that point. He enjoyed early success after joining a well-regarded law practice in town, but his partner, not he, had been the first to win a seat in Congress. In 1834, Lincoln had launched his own political career, but in the comparatively lowly position as a state legislator. In 1836, he gained reelection to the state house and then became the Whig Party's leader, where he led the charge to promote roads projects and other internal improvements in the state, along with the establishment of a state bank. All of these efforts, however, came to little avail by 1840 and, in the case of the bank, ended in complete collapse. The election of a Whig president that year might have buoyed his spirits, except for the fact that despite winning reelection himself, Lincoln failed in his leadership effort to carry Illinois for president-elect William Henry Harrison.

What was worse, in his love life Lincoln found no solace, only heartache, for even his happy courtship of the lovely, highly regarded, and well-heeled Whig doyenne Mary Todd turned to abject sadness when, in late 1840, at thirty-one years of age, he inexplicably broke off their marriage engagement. A melancholic soul by nature, Lincoln fell into the deepest depression of his life upon the dissolution of his relationship with Mary Todd. As he wrote in late January 1841, "I am now the most miserable man living. If what I feel were equally distributed to the whole human family, there would not be one cheerful face on the earth."[13] So deep was his despondency that Lincoln's roommate and best friend Joshua Speed claimed to have removed from their house all items Lincoln might use to harm himself—razors, knives, and the like.[14] Normally a man of his word, Lincoln's waffling on his commitment to wed Mary Todd left him jarred. Speaking of his resoluteness, Lincoln wrote to Speed in July 1842, "In that ability, you know, I once prided myself as the only, or at least the chief, gem of my character."[15] Whether he ultimately wed Mary out of care for reclaiming that gem, or because he felt he had found a treasure in her, it is hard to know. Evidence might point more to the former, as Lincoln's regard for loyalty was unquestioned by all who knew him well. He clearly possessed a capacity for deep feelings of love, as well, evidenced by the abyss into which he fell upon the much earlier death, in 1835, of Ann Rutledge, the object of his deep affection. With Mary Todd, it seems that the sentiment of duty in Abe may have been stronger than other considerations. She became his wife in November of 1842.

Neither marriage nor the birth of his first son, Robert Todd Lincoln, in 1843 could relieve in Lincoln a restlessness that, like his ambition, seemingly had no end. His bid to be the Whig Party's nominee for Congress in 1844 ended unsuccessfully. In 1846, he earned the nomination and then won the seat. While in office, he opposed the Mexican-American War. In a speech to the House of Representatives, Lincoln reflected on his own military service in the Black Hawk War of 1832:

> By the way Mr. Speaker, did you know that I am a military hero? Yes sir, in the days of the Black Hawk War I fought, bled and came away. . . . I was not at Stillman's defeat, but I was about as near it as Cass was Hull's surrender, and, like him, I saw the place very soon afterwards. . . . If he saw any live, fighting Indians, it was more than I did; but I had a good many bloody struggles with the mosquitoes, and although I never fainted from the loss of blood, I can truly say I was often very hungry.[16]

Lincoln's tenure in the House was as undistinguished as was his war record; he served only one term and chose not to stand for reelection in 1848.

Before he had turned thirty years of age, Alexander Hamilton had helped to establish the Bank of New York. At age thirty-three, Thomas Jefferson drafted the Declaration of Independence. George Washington was leading the Continental Army at forty-three. By that same age, in 1852, Abraham Lincoln had a small but successful law practice in the sleepy new capital city of one of the least populous states in the Union. He was not known nationally, and his life had been full of what seemed at times unmitigated sadness, for in addition to all of his other travails, in 1850, Lincoln had lost his second-born son, three-year-old Edward, to illness.

Hardship sometimes has a way of pressing humility on a person. The poverty into which Lincoln was born, and in which he languished for the first half of his life, made him more aware of its sting in the lives of others. The powerlessness he felt early in life, too, shaped his own conscience and heightened the attention he would show later in life to the plight of the powerless. His loss of love and loved ones reminded him of the even deeper loneliness suffered by widows and orphans. A constant concern in his political efforts from early on, when he called provision for the indigent "a legitimate end of government," and voted accordingly in the Illinois state legislature, Lincoln showed keen regard for the less fortunate in society. Nowhere was this clearer than in the case of enslaved Americans.

"BLOW OUT THE MORAL LIGHTS AROUND US"

Slavery, Lincoln stated with undeniable clarity throughout his life, was an abomination. With Lincoln's opposition to the institution of slavery having grown from his revulsion for the slave auctions he witnessed as a river boatman, he developed a thoroughgoing critique of slavery through moral reason. "As I would not be a slave, so I would not be a master," Lincoln said.[17] Logically, methodically, unswervingly, Lincoln challenged the underlying arguments and greed of the slaveholders. Citing his hero, the early nineteenth-century Whig statesman Henry Clay, Lincoln said that those who endorse slavery "blow out the moral lights around us."[18] Slavery violates the natural law, or moral order of the universe, and erases the idea of a common human nature. As an ideology that says, "You work, I eat," slavery quashes the soul of the slaves, mutilates their bodies, and treats human beings as if they were hogs.[19] Without showing any pity for the pathetic lot of slave masters, Lincoln also held that the institution of slavery corrupts slave owners even as it teaches their children and all others around them that might makes right. Ultimately, it makes republican—representative—government impossible.

Humility for Lincoln came first by hardship, then by habit. His early experiences without privilege, power, or prestige gave him an appreciation of how hard-won success is. It impelled him to fight so that others might have the opportunity he found. "Nowhere in the world," President Lincoln said in 1864 to the soldiers of an Ohio regiment, "is presented a government of so much liberty and equality. To the humblest and poorest amongst us are extended the highest privileges and positions. The present moment finds me at the White House, yet there is as good a chance for your children as there was for my father's."[20] Many people whose early path to power is full of hardship forget their early commitment to equality. Fond of the newfound perks of power, they are quick to publicly recall stories of their hardscrabble past, but then turn privately to their lives of luxury, with little regard for others who have nothing. Lincoln's path to power was unusual, for his humility grew as he became more powerful, almost as if the farther removed he found himself from his difficult past, the more humble he became. In his position of power, Lincoln's words in support of equality, opportunity, and mercy were matched by actions on behalf of these principles—and for the people denied equality, opportunity, and liberty for far too long.

The Civil War was fought to preserve the Union and to end slavery. It came, Lincoln said in his Second Inaugural Address, despite the fact that "both sides deprecated war; but one of them would make war rather than let the nation survive; and the other would accept war rather than let it perish."[21] Regardless of his protestations to the contrary, Lincoln was accused then, and is still accused now, of visiting war upon the nation. Throughout his time as president, there was never a day when criticism of this sort, or some other, did not rain down upon him. Frederick Douglass noted this constant deluge against Lincoln in an 1876 speech marking the installation, in Washington, D.C., of a statue depicting the Great Emancipator along with freed slaves:

Few great public men have ever been the victims of fiercer denunciation than Abraham Lincoln was during his administration. He was often wounded in the house of his friends. Reproaches came thick and fast upon him from within and from without, and from opposite quarters. He was assailed by Abolitionists; he was assailed by slaveholders; he was assailed by the men were for peace at any price; he was assailed by those were for a more prosecution of the war; he was assailed for not making the war an abolition war; and he was bitterly assailed for making the war an abolition war.[22]

Lincoln's navigation of these almost impossible waters was not without mistakes. What distinguished him from many others, however, were his ability to shift his course without ever losing sight of his destination and his willingness to admit when he steered awry.

Statesmanship has often been compared to captaining a ship. This may be the best way to understand this art, but for Lincoln, the body of water with which he was most familiar—the Mississippi River—required a pilot of a ship to move from place to place across the river. All the while, the pilot knew he had to go downstream, but he did not dare take on much more than what was before him. Lincoln's own approach to the immensely complex questions of statecraft leading up to and during the Civil War mirrored the way he had approached lesser political problems earlier in his career— always with a deliberate decision-making process that led some of his opponents, and even some of his friends, as Frederick Douglass noted, to accuse him of intentional delay.

Of all the areas of Lincoln's wartime statesmanship that drew harsh criticism, two marked the roughest waters: the question of emancipation and his handling of Union generals. Often these two currents converged, creating some of the most turbulent spots of his presidency. Lincoln had to helm the Union, he believed, to a much safer and freer place. The aims of the war were intertwined in his mind: preserve the Union and end slavery. While Lincoln's moral opposition to slavery had been constant in the decades before the 1861 start of the Civil War, his awareness of the enormity of the crisis was awakened in the 1850s with a series of political and constitutional decisions that, taken together, Lincoln saw as an outright assault on the principles of the Declaration of Independence and the Constitution. While most abolitionists during this crucial time, including influential leaders like New Englanders William Lloyd Garrison and Wendell Phillips, saw the Constitution—because they believed it sanctioned slavery—as an impediment to their goal of ending the institution, Lincoln maintained that unless Americans stand on the Constitution, the forces of slaveholding would prevail. Most abolitionists saw Lincoln's position, which would eliminate slavery only in the federally controlled territories, as a blood-soaked bargain. Forget the Constitution, they said, since it does not allow congressional or presidential action to end slavery in states that allowed it.

Make the moral argument against slavery, Lincoln responded, by all means, but unless it be buttressed by a constitutional argument for its abolition, there will be nothing left on which he could stand. Biblical principles comport with slavery's abolition, Lincoln held, but the Bible should not be used as a trump card to the Constitution, as some abolitionists urged, advocating the position that God's law, not man's law, should prevail when they are in conflict. Man's law is wrong, Lincoln admitted, insofar as slavery is sanctioned, but it must be changed through means set up in the Constitution, or else the country will be left without a rudder. The president, Lincoln believed, both before and during the time he held the office, was powerless to unilaterally eliminate slavery from the states. Abolitionist legislators, too, were bound by the Constitution. In claiming that its strictures were superseded by divine law, abolitionists thought their actions courageous. In fact, they were rash and, as Lincoln argued, ended up endangering the republic.

Just as Lincoln's position on slavery dissatisfied the abolitionists and radical Republicans, so too did it frustrate many others who thought him too hard on the institution, including many Democrats. Ease up, said Democratic Illinois senator Stephen A. Douglas, whom Lincoln unsuccessfully challenged in 1858, and let the people in each territory decide the matter. Calling their position "popular sovereignty," Douglas Democrats, Lincoln came to believe, were in favor of more than a simple up or down vote on slavery in the territories. By refusing to stand up against the immorality of slavery, Douglas Democrats, Lincoln alleged, would have the effect of encouraging its expansion into the territories. In so doing, they fell in line with those proslavery forces who believed that slavery would be saved in the East as the United States pushed farther west.

By the mid-1850s, powerful factions within Lincoln's Whig Party had drifted into agreement with Douglas. An upstart party, the Republicans, came out with a platform in 1854 saying that the principles of the American founding entailed but one conclusion: slavery's expansion into the territories must not be tolerated. In 1856, Lincoln left the Whigs, and in 1858, he ran as a Republican against Douglas in the United States Senate race in Illinois. With abolitionists to one side and expansionists to the other, Lincoln was navigating down a fast-moving river surrounded by political foes eager to see him fail.

By steering a course between slave abolitionism and expansionism, Lincoln was not playing it cautiously, afraid to take a risk. His

ABRAHAM LINCOLN

prudence was not timidity. Rather, his actions embodied the classical definition of prudence as practical wisdom or the seeking of a just end through the achievement of the right means. Cleverness, on the other hand, confuses means and ends and does not care about the moral force of either. Humility is a virtue prerequisite to prudence. If one lacks humility, the advancement of self or the substitution of an immoral end can overwhelm the pursuit of a just end. This arrogance marked the presidency of Lincoln's predecessor in the White House, James Buchanan, who made the disastrously immoral decision that the problem of slavery would go away with the Supreme Court's decision in *Dred Scott* in 1857. His middle course was monstrous, in fact, for in failing to confront the worst decision ever issued by the Supreme Court, which held that a black man was neither a man nor a citizen in the United States, he greatly aided and abetted the slave cause. Lincoln, incensed at Buchanan's moral turpitude, denounced him as part of a conspiracy to keep slavery alive in America. If an immoral end or one's own aggrandizement is substituted for a just end, the strategic and tactical path chosen will be a meandering one. Prudence allows the statesman to consider all alternatives and to make a decision not based upon who garners glory but upon the proper demands of the situation at hand. Prudence requires the submersion of one's ego.

"GOD HAS DECIDED THIS QUESTION"

When it came to his relationship with his generals, Lincoln was then and now portrayed as indecisive, even incorrigibly slow to act. During the war, the fulminations against him came quick and steady, as many military men and civilian critics alike were ready to offer their opinions about what Lincoln should do. It took him too long, many charged, to get Ulysses S. Grant into place heading the army.

Lincoln's first choice, George McClellan, was no good. Just how awful he was, however, was not revealed until July 1862, when he handed Lincoln a letter during the president's visit to the Army of the Potomac at Harrison's Landing on the James River, in eastern Virginia, not too far from Williamsburg. In his letter to the commander in chief, General McClellan laid out his case as to why slavery should be left alone, and other Confederate property, as he saw it, left unseized as well. "A system of policy thus constitutional and conservative, and pervaded by the influences of Christianity and freedom, would receive the support of almost all truly loyal men, would deeply impress the rebel masses and all foreign nations, and it might be humbly hoped that it would commend itself to the favor of the Almighty." If Lincoln were to emancipate the slaves, McClellan wrote, it would be tantamount to a "radical" policy that would make army recruitment "almost hopeless." McClellan not only announced his uninvited views to his superior; he also acted on them, offering through his aide what amounted to an offer of settlement with the South. Upon the completion of this treaty, what he hoped would be a "coup," McClellan, arrogant to the end, bragged, "My enemies will be at my feet."[23]

McClellan's demands of Lincoln were prompted by the possibility that Lincoln would free the slaves. Adamant in his conviction that he lacked the constitutional power to do so unilaterally, Lincoln nonetheless knew that emancipation as a military measure was a very different thing. An executive order affecting areas of combat was within the purview of the commander in chief, whereas an edict issued by the president on nonmilitary grounds was beyond the constitutional scope of his power. To stay true to his constitutional convictions, as well as do justice to the cause of the slaves, Lincoln decided in his own mind that if the time came—after a victory by the Union army, say—he would issue a proclamation of emancipation for slaves living in areas controlled by the Union army. Having come to this decision much later than many abolitionists had urged, Lincoln knew that if ever he announced his decision, the reaction would be swift and furious—even from within his own party.

Humility is not headstrong; nor is it hapless. It is not passive but strong. Avoiding rashness himself, Lincoln exercised a deliberateness of thought and action that, however much it sometimes made him seem indecisive, in fact proved over and over again a boon to the ends he sought. His mighty effort to win over those in his own circle to the justice of emancipating slaves is one example of this. While McClellan and others in 1862 criticized the president, anticipating antislavery actions from Lincoln that they felt would antagonize certain factions in the North, many other radical Republicans at the same time were urging the president to do more against slavery.

On September 4, 1862, the Army of Northern Virginia, led by Robert E. Lee and buoyed by a series of triumphs over Union forces, launched an invasion of Maryland. (It was this northern thrust that led Lincoln to elevate George C. McClellan as commander of the Army of the Potomac.) The clash of the armies came on what we now call Constitution Day—September 17, 1862. Few would have time in 1862 to pause and remember the concluding day of the 1787 Constitutional Convention, when the document was signed, but nevertheless all knew that the fate of the Union hung in the balance. As Benjamin Franklin said on that day in 1787, "It's a republic, if you can keep it."[24]

Keeping the republic, and the Union, would claim more than twenty-six thousand casualties from both armies at Antietam. It was the bloodiest day of the war. To this day, it is the bloodiest day in American history. And owing to McClellan's intransigent inaction, it decided next to nothing. Finally, more than a month and a half after Antietam, Lincoln fired the "Young Napoleon." At the same time Lincoln lamented the missed opportunity at Antietam, he also knew that Lee thereafter would be on the run. While not really a victory, Antietam was also not enough of a blow to derail Lincoln's plans for issuing a proclamation to free the slaves in Confederate territory controlled by Union forces. A kind of divine prompt, Lincoln claimed, along with the victory at Antietam, gave him the go-ahead on the Emancipation Proclamation. Antietam, however awful the battle, provided just enough of a break for the Union. As Lincoln said upon announcing the Proclamation to his cabinet on September 22, 1862, "God has decided this question in favor of the slaves."[25] Scheduled to take effect January 1, 1863, the Emancipation Proclamation was a courageous step.

For some, it was not bold enough. Most abolitionists said that Lincoln's decision came too late and offered too little. The president should free all the slaves, not just those in Southern states controlled by the Union army. There was dissension even in the president's own cabinet, which was not given nearly as much power as its members would like. In part to remedy this problem and stock the cabinet with more of their own, in December 1862, the radical Republicans, who outnumbered the Democrats in the Senate nearly two to one, tried to impose what amounted to a "cabinet council" on Lincoln. By this innovation, which would mean that they would control the president's cabinet picks, they sought a cabinet that would act in lockstep with their own desires for total war—and total war on slavery. "Too weak," they said of Lincoln's attacks on the South (their charge came after the Union's disastrous mid-December defeat at Fredericksburg), and "too slow," they said of his actions against slavery. In general, they charged him with being an anemic executive. Even though by this time he had announced his intention to issue the final Emancipation Proclamation in less than two weeks, Lincoln was assailed by the radicals as insufficiently committed to the cause of ending slavery. In effect, they were giving their leader a vote of no confidence.

Having called the radicals' leadership to a meeting on December 18, 1862, Lincoln proceeded to school them on the reason their efforts to impose a council on the president were more befitting a parliamentary form of government than their own. He was the president, and it was important for him to hear dissenting voices within his own cabinet. If they should wish to make it into a univocal voice, what good would it be? Although it took a meeting of some five hours in length, Lincoln repelled what could have been a catastrophic coup.

Lincoln's commitment to hearing all sides, even when they disagreed with him, owed its existence to an admirable intellectual humility. This humility helped him miss the river shoals that otherwise would have run his administration aground, as well as the country. Had he given himself over to either side—the Douglas Democrats or the radical Republicans—the goal of emancipation might not have been achieved. To precipitously pursue that course, without having engaged the other side who so strongly opposed emancipation, might have meant that the coalition that was needed to carry off the plan never would have been forged.

Once having secured victory in war, Lincoln knew that even rougher postwar waters were ahead. Calling the task of reintegrating the Southern states into the Union "the greatest question ever presented to practical statesmanship," Lincoln had to combat radicals committed to a very different course.[26] Their Reconstruction of the South, sadly, absent his statesmanship, lacked both humility and justice in its harsh, punitive measures. Having ignored the plea for charity Lincoln made before his death, the radical Republicans withheld both the generosity and the mercy that might have been at the heart of Lincoln's Reconstruction efforts.

"RIGHT, AS GOD GIVES US TO SEE THE RIGHT"

Thomas Aquinas noted that the virtue of prudence is related to the idea of Providence in that both are concerned with a correct ordering of things.[27] Even as Abraham Lincoln had a deepening sense of the powerless as he grew more powerful, so too, as the pressures mounted on him, did he come to a deeper sense of the divine. This was no foxhole conversion, however, for Lincoln never enmeshed himself into organized religion. Rather, for Lincoln, it appeared that as inexplicable as God's ways were to human beings, it was even more inexplicable to suppose that human beings just carried on without God ever intervening in our affairs. "God governs in the affairs of man," Benjamin Franklin had told the delegates of the Constitutional Convention in 1787.[28] Like Franklin, Lincoln believed that God was active not only in the lives of individuals but of nations as well. But how do we know what he wants us to do? As Lincoln wrote in a private memo preserved by his secretary, "The will of God prevails. In great contests each party claims to act in accordance with the will of God. Both may be, and one must be, wrong. . . . In the present civil war it is quite possible that God's purpose is something different from the purpose of either party; and yet the human instrumentalities, working just as they do, are of the adaptation to effect his purpose. . . ."[29] In this document, what Lincoln called "The Meditation on the Divine Will," dated September 30, 1862, and secreted away for his private, not public, purposes, Lincoln outlined his thoughts on God and the war about a month before he sent a late-October missive to Eliza Gurney.

A faithful correspondent despite all of his presidential duties, Lincoln penned a letter in response to Gurney, a Quaker who had written him what amounted to a sermon leading up to a prayer that God would grant the president wisdom. In his short letter to Gurney, he reflected on his role in the war, and God's role in the world, beginning with the declaration, "We are indeed going through a great trial—a fiery trial." Proceeding then to admit that his "position" was a "very responsible one," Lincoln identified himself as "a humble instrument in the hands of our Heavenly Father." As such, he had to act "to work out his great purposes . . . according to his will." If Lincoln were to fail, he wrote, it would have been "for some purpose unknown to me," but by God's will. Why God allowed the war to continue when Lincoln wished that it had never started was fathomable only by "some purpose of [God's] own, mysterious and unknown to us." Reemphasizing our limits next to God's, Lincoln said that although "with our limited understandings we may not be able to comprehend it, yet we cannot but believe, that he who made the world still governs it."[30]

Lincoln had used the evocative phrase to refer to himself, "a humble instrument in the hands of our Heavenly Father," once before, in February 1861. In an address to the New Jersey Senate in Trenton, Lincoln stated, "I shall be most happy indeed if I shall be a humble instrument in the hands of the Almighty, and of this, his almost chosen people, for perpetuating the object of that great struggle."[31]

When we pick up a Civil War historical novel today or flip on a cable documentary about the conflict, we can rest easy about the outcome. We know the winner. Lincoln had no such luxury. Throughout much of the war, he thought all was lost. Humility helped keep him from despairing, for it pushed his trust back to his belief that God had a plan, even if it was nearly impossible for human beings to understand it.

It is hard to say at what point in the war Lincoln felt the most sadness—for there were many such moments—but close to the bottom, surely, was the death of his beloved son Willie. In late January or early February 1862, the Lincolns' eleven-year-old son, Willie, contracted typhoid fever from fetid water piped into the White House from a nearby polluted canal. The president and First Lady, distraught at the thought of losing their son, who had been born less than a year after they had lost Edward, remained with their boy, bedside. Named after Edward's attending physician, Willie was the apple of his father's eye. Having seen the methodical way Willie approached a problem, Lincoln said of his son, "I know every step of the process by which that boy arrived at his satisfactory solution of the question before him, as it is by just such slow methods I attain results."[32] Willie died on February 20, 1862. His inconsolable mother could not even attend her boy's funeral. Elizabeth Keckley, a former slave who became Mary Todd Lincoln's personal seamstress and close associate, helped the Lincolns through this awful time. She described Lincoln's reaction to Willie's death: "Great sobs choked his utterance. He buried his head in his hands, his tall frame was convulsed with emotion. . . . His grief unnerved him, and made him a weak, passive child. I did not dream that his rugged nature could be so moved."[33] Lincoln's secretary, John Nicolay, recorded the president's words, "Well, Nicolay, my boy is gone—he is actually gone!"[34]

After the death of Willie, a downward spiral of sadness gripped the president and his wife. Death, it seemed—of young Americans in the tens of thousands, and now his son—was all he knew. As the historian Allen Guelzo reminds us, there was, according to Lincoln's own account, "a tired spot in him that no rest could ever touch."[35] At the start of the war, the sixteenth president was fifty-two years old. He looked angular as he always had but also "erect and powerful," as Guelzo describes him. Still, as he also notes, "But by the end of the war, Lincoln's face had grown aged and care-worn, his cheeks sunken into ashen hollows, his coarse black hair showing tufts of white, and his beard shrunken to a pitiful tuft at the chin."[36]

We can only wonder what it felt like for Lincoln to feel his soul grow weary along with his body. It is a weary yet resplendent soul that is revealed in Lincoln's letter to Eliza Gurney. While Lincoln talked of "a fiery trial" and of an ineffable God who controls history, he was also able still to speak of his "very responsible position." The upshot of Lincoln's admission is that despite the fact that he "happen[ed] to be placed" in that "very responsible position," he took responsibility nonetheless.[37] But what responsibility was left to Lincoln, we might ask, given Lincoln's presentation of a providential God whose ways seemed willful, even inscrutable?

Humility for Lincoln was tied directly to man's relationship to the Almighty. In Lincoln's humility, perhaps more powerfully than in that of any other figure, we see the spiritual dimension of this great virtue. As he described himself in the Gurney letter, Lincoln was "a humble instrument in the hands of our Heavenly Father." In the hands of his earthly father, Lincoln had known only rough treatment. Imperious and uneducated, Thomas Lincoln was a hard man. As was customary for indigent backwoods families of the early nineteenth century, for Abe's first twenty-one years, he was completely at the whim of his father's dictates. For young Abe, this meant hard labor. This early experience, combined with the austere Calvinism of his mother's religious convictions, colored Lincoln's idea of divine fatherhood. But while his experience with his own father might have helped shape his view of God, Lincoln's mature political thought was carefully honed and had a theological richness unrivaled in American history.

Abraham Lincoln demonstrated that humility gives us eyes to see that we are not God. God may seem distant, perhaps even ultimately unknowable. But even if God is ineffable, he is not unjust.

And even if he is omnipotent, he is not irresponsible. Lincoln knew that he was not a purely passive "instrument." God's power never divests us of responsibility. Humility is not inaction combined with hope that things will work out. However much Abraham Lincoln spoke of himself as a "humble instrument in the hands of God," he never lapsed into inactivity.

Passivity leads to despair, but so does unchecked pride. In the midst of his "fiery trials," Lincoln staved off utter despair with the recognition that he was responsible to his fellow citizens, to the Constitution, and ultimately, to God. Lincoln was responsible to a people he so revered that he deemed them "almost chosen."[38] His humility in his task helped him stave off self-pity. As the twentieth-century monk Thomas Merton wrote, self-pity cannot exist where there is humility.[39] Pride left unchecked breeds self-pity, for once the strivings of the arrogant man prove futile, his only refuge is self-pity. Humility lets the theological virtue of hope shine brightly.

In the history of great oratory there is no more hopeful, and yet no more sorrowful, speech than Abraham Lincoln's Second Inaugural Address, delivered in January 1865, just four months before the end of the war. In Lincoln's "Meditation on the Divine Will," as with his letter to Eliza Gurney, he stated that it is our task to conform our ways to God's. It is not for us to speak for God. This humble realization, one that Lincoln lived throughout his life, came into the fullness of his intellectual, moral, and political reasoning with his Second Inaugural Address. Its echo is heard throughout that address, in which Lincoln reflected upon the will of the Lord and the responsibility of the people.

"The Almighty has his own purposes," Lincoln said halfway

through his address. And then, quoting from Matthew's gospel, Lincoln said, "'Woe unto the world because of offences! For it must needs be that offences come; but woe to that man by whom the offence cometh.'" Slavery can be supposed to be among those offences, Lincoln stated, and the war to end it was due "by whom the offence came." This realization did not mean, Lincoln quickly added, that they should welcome the war. "Fondly do we hope— fervently do we pray—that this mighty scourge of war may speedily pass away." If it did not immediately pass, and "every drop of blood drawn by the lash shall be paid by another drawn by the sword," Lincoln said, we must conclude that, as was said in the Psalms, "The judgments of the Lord are true and righteous altogether."[40]

Lincoln's curious choice of quotation from the New Testament gospel of Matthew captures Jesus' words in response to a question posed to him by a disciple. That question was, "Who is the greatest in the kingdom of heaven?" The response by Jesus was to call forth a child and admonish the adults to be more like the little one: "Therefore, whoever humbles himself like this child is the greatest in the kingdom of heaven" (Matt. 18:1, 3–4 NIV). To cause a child to sin is an offense worthy of death. "Woe to the world because of the things that cause people to sin! Such things must come, but woe to the man through whom they come!" Jesus said (Matt. 18:7 NIV). To be the greatest, you must be the most humble. In the aftermath of the war, Lincoln urged humility for both the North and the South— not just about what God would have them do, but how they should act toward each other.

Even after the great losses in his life, and the near death of the Union he loved, Lincoln came to the realization that however distant or inscrutable God might seem to be, he does not give up on justice. Lincoln closed his address with a challenge to the American people:

> With malice toward none; with charity for all; with firmness in the right, as God gives us to see the right, let us strive on to finish the work we are in; to bind up the nation's wounds; to care for him who shall have borne battle, and for his widow, and his orphan—to do all which may achieve and cherish a just and lasting peace among ourselves, and with all nations.[41]

This is a summons to all human beings to chasten their pride. Act with intellectual humility, he said, or a willingness to admit when you are wrong. Act with spiritual humility, not presuming that your ways are God's. Seek his wisdom in what you do. Act firmly for the right. Put aside malice, Lincoln said, and put on charity. A child is exemplary of humility, Jesus said, in words that Lincoln took to heart. A child, Lincoln knew, perhaps thinking of Willie, or Edward, or the thousands of boys and girls left orphaned by the Civil War, is the greatest in the kingdom of heaven. Not the powerful or the prestigious or those puffed up with pride—but a child.

EIGHT

FREDERICK DOUGLASS

rederick Douglass was among the tens of thousands of Americans who braved bad weather on a muddy March day in 1865 to hear Abraham Lincoln's Second Inaugural Address. Denied entry to the postinaugural reception because he was black, Douglass petitioned the president for entry. Lincoln immediately had him escorted into the White House. "Here comes my friend," Lincoln said, seeing Douglass approach. Asked by the president his opinion of the Second Inaugural Address, the ex-slave, abolitionist leader, orator, and statesman said, "Mr. Lincoln, that was a sacred effort."[1] It was the last time the two men would see each other.

Their previous meeting, in 1864, had a somber agenda. Wondering what might come of slaves in the South if his efforts to win the war would fail, Lincoln called for Douglass so they could discuss the matter. In his meeting with Lincoln, Douglass was impressed both by the respect he was shown and the "deep moral conviction" the president maintained about the issue. "In his company," Douglass stated of Lincoln, "I was never in any way reminded of my humble origin, or of my unpopular color."[2] Reminiscent of their first meeting in August 1863, about which Douglass said he was received "just as you have seen one gentleman receive another," the reception Lincoln offered Douglass in 1864 had a lasting impact.[3] The three occasions on which they met were markedly different from so many of the other meetings Douglass had had with well-intentioned whites. Whereas many others with whom Douglass had met, even those in the abolitionist movement, treated him with condescension, Lincoln made him feel proud to be who he was. A proud man—and a humble one—Frederick Douglass shared with Abraham Lincoln the lack of arrogance that made them both effective advocates for liberty. Beyond anything Lincoln ever endured, however, Douglass came to his pride—and his humility—by overcoming the humiliation of slavery.

"SLAVERY IN ITS TRUE COLOR"

In the same year in which Illinois became a state, and in which Abraham Lincoln's mother died, Frederick Douglass was born. He never knew for sure the day of his birth or the month; for a while he was even unsure about the year. His best guess was that he was born in February 1818. Officially, his mother named him Frederick Augustus Washington Bailey. He later used the surname Stanley, then Johnson, and then, finally, Douglass, after the lead character (plus an added "s" at the end) in Sir Walter Scott's poem "Lady of the

Lake." He did not know the identity of his father, but it was probably his first master, Aaron Anthony, a white man who served as chief overseer of properties for Colonel Edward Lloyd, one of Maryland's wealthiest men. Young Freddy hardly knew his mother, who lived on a neighboring farm, and she died before he turned eight years old.

His early life was full of near nakedness, hunger, and constant weariness. With the sun beating down on their backs in the summer and frost nipping their fingers in the winter, slaves on the eastern shore of Maryland endured harsh conditions in the large plantation community into which Frederick was born. Loneliness was his only constant companion for much of his childhood. Falling to his hands and knees to retrieve the crumbs that were dropped on the floor before the household dogs and cats could get to them, Douglass was often reduced to animal existence. Humiliation was heaped upon humiliation in his early life, much of it by masters who professed a love of God. His early years, he wrote later in one of the three autobiographies he penned, were "without an intelligible beginning."[4]

What relationships young Fred had were full of strife. Among the five hundred slaves housed on the Lloyd properties was one known to the boy as "Aunt Katy." Despite being a slave herself, Aunt Katy was entrusted by the plantation overseer with supervision of many household duties, including those of the kitchen. According to Frederick's account, Aunt Katy often singled him out for punishment. Having been deprived of even his meager daily allowance of food one day, and having been told by Aunt Katy that she "would starve the life out of [him]," Frederick was shocked to find his mother enter the room. As she overheard the abuse, Frederick noted "a deep and tender pity" in his mother's glance his way, and then "fiery indignation" directed toward his tormentor. For Frederick, it was one of the first times anyone had risen to his defense. "That night," he later wrote, "I learned as I had never learned before, that I was not only a child, but somebody's child. I was grander upon my mother's knee than a king upon his throne."[5] Having walked thirteen miles to see him upon the conclusion of her workday, Frederick's mother had to walk the same distance back to her home during that night, a full marathon of maternal love. Frederick's feeling of belonging was short-lived, as it was the last time he ever saw his mother. In honor of the date of that last visit, Douglass later decided that he would celebrate his birthday each year on February 14.

According to the mature Frederick Douglass, slavery was best summarized as tyranny. Within slavery's system, masters knew their "property" were people but had to do everything in their power to deny that reality. Marriages among slaves were dissolved and spouses separated, parents and children often were split apart, and love affairs between slaves were strictly forbidden. The resulting dehumanization of slaves was an assault on all of human nature, for in degrading the slaves the masters sank further into vice. The rapes, beatings, and overall brutality, plus the prospect that any slave could be sold away to an even worse fate at any time, made their existence the same as that of subjects of a capricious tyrant. Liberty looked like an impossibly distant goal. About the opposition between masters and slaves, Douglass reflected, "There was pride, pomp, and luxury on the one hand, servility, dejection, and misery on the other."[6]

Slavery was a self-perpetuating cycle of disordered pride and

debased conduct. The "soul-crushing and death-dealing character of slavery" was given rise to by an arrogance that wishes others
to work for one's own gain.[7] Humiliation is the means by which
this end is accomplished. Douglass witnessed no more harrow-
ing example of humiliation than Colonel Lloyd's whipping of Old
Barney, a slave who was about as old as his imperious owner. "These
two men were both advanced in years; there were the silver locks of
the master, and the bald and toil-worn brow of the slave—superior
and inferior here, powerful and weak here, but *equals* before God."[8]
Old Barney, described by Douglass as possessing "a respectful and
dignified bearing," was the keeper of the Lloyd stable, along with his
son, Young Barney. Obsessed with his horses, Lloyd was always find-
ing fault with their care. After noting some perceived infraction of
the stable rules by Old Barney, Lloyd ordered the old slave to kneel.
Lloyd then delivered thirty lashes with his horsewhip. Douglass had
watched countless whippings, but at this one he was "shocked" to
see "the spectacle of an aged man—a husband and a father—humbly
kneeling before his fellow-man," taking the lashes "patiently," with
"no resistance," responding to "each blow with only a shrug of the
shoulders and a groan."[9] What young Freddy Bailey witnessed in that
incident, he later said, was "slavery in its true color."[10]

The attempted humiliation of Old Barney helped demonstrate
to Douglass that slavery was an ideology that was dependent upon
the humiliation of others to survive. Slavery gained strength mainly
at the expense of its victims. The self-interest of the slaveholders grew
as they discovered how good it was to watch the slaves do their work.
Who would relinquish such a life? To enslave another is to forget
one's own limits. From Douglass's position, slave masters and those

who stood for slavery did not recognize the limits of nature, God, or good government. Many in mid-nineteenth-century America, in fact, began to call slavery a "positive good." Often built on religious ideology that supposed whites blessed on account of their blood and blacks cursed because of their lineage, those who saw slavery as a good for slaves, as well as for masters, often cited pseudoscience to buttress their religious argument. Claiming that the native intellect of blacks precluded their being anything other than slaves, the positive good school said that the slaves' rescue from Africa saved their lives and that the slaves' introduction to Christianity saved their souls. Slaves should be grateful to their masters. Against this foul ideology Douglass invoked common sense. "There is not a man beneath the canopy of heaven that does not know that slavery is wrong for *him,*" Douglass said.[11] If slavery is such a good thing, Douglass was asking, why does no one volunteer to be a slave? Positive-gooders are self-deluded and believe that they will never be confronted by the lie that is at the heart of their ideology. They would not wish to be slaves, and know it, yet they wish to enslave others and call it good.

Douglass could conclude only that such a perverse view of the world was borne of hubris. Just as the ancient Greeks believed that hubris, or arrogance, would meet its fate at the hands of Nemesis, or the goddess of revenge, so too did Douglass adopt a similar view in his articulation of America's original sin. The arrogance of the slave interests resulted in the comeuppance of civil war. "At last our proud Republic is overtaken," he wrote in a piece called "Nemesis," a month after the start of the Civil War, in May 1861. "Our National Sin has found us out. The National Head is bowed down, and our face is mantled with shame and confusion." We could not blame any

desirous of an education. Taking his master's words at their face value, Frederick set out to prove them right. If it is true, he thought, that "knowledge unfits a child to be a slave," then knowledgeable and unfit he would become![16]

Frederick threw himself wholeheartedly into his project for self-enlightenment. His search for more knowledge awakened in him an ever-growing "love of liberty."[17] At the age of thirteen, Frederick bought a book, paid for out of his boot-blacking earnings, that would help to change his life. Called *The Columbian Orator*, the "rich treasure" of a volume contained some of the great oratory of the Western world, including speeches by Socrates, the Roman statesman Cato the Younger, and George Washington, among many others. What touched Frederick the most was a dialogue between a master and a slave in which the slave bests the master at every point in a debate about the justice of slavery, at which point the master, in a turn unlikely to transpire in real life, granted the slave his freedom and sent him on his way. "Here indeed was a noble acquisition," Frederick said of his book. "I had now penetrated to the secret of all slavery and of all oppression, and had ascertained their true foundation to be in the pride, the power and the avarice of man."[18] No longer cowed by those who claimed God was on their side in the debate over slavery, Frederick resolved to free himself and his fellow slaves from their attitude of submission. "Light had penetrated the moral dungeon where I had lain," he later reflected.[19] Hugh Auld's warning to his wife proved more prophetic than ever he anticipated, as Frederick, having found knowledge of another way of living, could not abide continued enslavement.

Frederick's enlightenment brought relief to him, not least of which was the realization that Christianity need not be identified with the slaveholding interest. Casting his cares upon God in a way that previously he had been unable to do, the teenaged Frederick came to Christ with the help of an older man whose life was one of prayer. While Uncle Lawson taught Frederick "the spirit," or how to live in God, Frederick in turn taught his elder the "letter" of things, or how to read. In this exchange, Uncle Lawson became a kind of spiritual father to Frederick. Enlightened by learning, Frederick's heart was lit on fire for God and also for the good that he might do for his fellow men. Uncle Lawson, Frederick later wrote, "fanned my already intense love of knowledge into a flame by assuring me that I was to be a useful man in the world."[20] At first doubtful that a slave could amount to anything in life, Frederick learned from Lawson to trust in God. He did so and found a peace that had up to that time in his young life eluded him.

Frederick's internal peace did not bring an end to the disorder around him. Occasionally sent back to the eastern shore of Maryland to work for Thomas Auld, Douglass was keen to try his hand at teaching, an effort that would allow him to share his faith and his learning. "Here," he later wrote, "is something worth living for." As Douglass led a Sunday reading class for his fellow slaves, Thomas Auld and some others, fearing that the teaching would unleash a longing for liberty, "rushed in upon [the group] with sticks and stones, and broke [the] virtuous little Sabbath school, at St. Michael's—all calling themselves Christians! Humble followers of the Lord Jesus Christ!"[21] That Thomas claimed to be a newly converted Christian made this experience all that much more confounding for Douglass.

Frederick began to see the power of humility through lessons learned in his early life. Whether by negative examples (his masters and mistresses and slave interests throughout his life) or positive examples (his mother and Uncle Lawson), Frederick saw what it took to be humble even in the midst of humiliation. Submission of one sort was thrust upon him as a slave, but before he could escape the bonds of slavery, Frederick had to make himself a student. His humility as a learner was preparation for his life as a leader. In humbling himself as a seeker, he gained the pride and dignity that unfitted him for slavery. The arrogance of those who wished to break Frederick was no match for his combination of healthy pride in himself and humility before his mission.

"FREEMAN IN FACT, SLAVE IN FORM"

In Frederick's case, those who wished to break him wanted to do so literally. With his behavior becoming more and more rebellious in the eyes of his master, Thomas Auld, who had scuttled the Sunday school for slaves, Frederick was finally sent away to Edward Covey, the area's most infamous slave-breaker. The men involved in the slave-breaking business were especially hard-hearted, and Covey was no exception, despite the fact that he tried to hide behind a pious religious exterior. Pledged to Covey for a full year, Frederick entered his new captivity with dread. "There was neither joy in my heart nor elasticity in my frame as I started for the tyrant's home," he later recalled.[22] On his seven-mile walk to Covey's, Frederick, only sixteen, reflected on how much his own life was subject to the whims of others. Where would he end up?

Covey lost little time in beating the boy. Just three days after Frederick's arrival, he already had "wales" on his back as large as his little finger.[23] Again and again his accounts of slaveholders to which he was subject, Douglass used the word *proud* or some variation of it to describe them. It was as if the viciousness of their trade became etched on their faces, readily visible to all who encountered them. Of Covey, in particular, Douglass later wrote, "Cold, distant, morose, with a face wearing all the marks of captious pride and malicious sternness, he repelled all advances."[24] The "pride," or arrogance, of the slaveholders could not have been more opposed to the "pride," or dignity, Frederick gained as he came closer to securing his freedom. The evil pride of his masters—foul, furious, and built on nothing noble—was in stark contrast to the healthy pride into which Douglass grew, thought by thought and step by step. Spiritually, intellectually, and physically, Douglass was gaining in the pride that would give him the strength to find his freedom.

At first, Covey relished his success in breaking Frederick, "in body, soul, and spirit," as Douglass later said.[25] The slave's first task, taking a team of oxen to the field, proved a disaster and provoked a string a beatings from Covey that continued weekly for some six months. For Frederick, the lesson learned from the incident with the oxen was not so much physical as existential: "They were property; so was I. Covey was to break me—I was to break them. Break and be broken was the order."[26] After that incident and more like it in subsequent days, Douglass's doubts about whether he would ever be free made him conclude, "I would have exchanged my manhood for the brutehood of an ox."[27]

Unrelenting work was Covey's rule and Frederick's fate. As

Douglass recollected of his master, "The longest days were too short for him, and the shortest nights were too long for him."[28] Thoughts of suicide and homicide crossed Frederick's mind, but a "combination of hope and fear" kept him from taking his own life or that of Covey. Ships passing in the Chesapeake Bay caused him to cry out for freedom. As he later admitted, "I was completely wrecked, changed, and bewildered; goaded almost to madness at one time, and at another reconciling myself to my wretched condition."[29]

Douglass, the mature man who wrote his third and final autobiography, the *Life and Times of Frederick Douglass*, in 1881, looked back at the second half of his wretched time under Covey and wrote that he had been "humbled, degraded, broken down, enslaved, and brutalized."[30] Douglass used a similar description in his second autobiography, *My Bondage and My Freedom*, which he wrote when he was thirty-seven years old and published in 1855. His first account of his life, *Narrative of the Life of Frederick Douglass, An American Slave*, was published only seven years after he gained his freedom, in 1845, and as a result gave a shorter account of his time with Covey, for fear that he might still be pursued as a fugitive. It did not include the phrase he had used to describe his life under Covey ("humbled, degraded, broken down, enslaved, and brutalized") that he used in his latter two accounts, but in its stead it included the following two sentences: "The circumstances leading to the change in Mr. Covey's course toward me form an epoch in my humble history. You have seen how a man was made a slave; you shall see how a slave was made a man."[31]

Humility is a great virtue—something to be desired, cultivated, and even won through hard-fought struggles. But for Douglass, especially in his early life, it certainly was difficult for him to see how *humility* was something to be sought, for *humiliation* was pressed on him from all sides. For Douglass, it is therefore understandable why his use of the word *humble* in his own account of his life often has the meaning of "being humiliated." It recalls the literal, not the strong, quality of humility as it relates to the ground, the *humus*. In his young life, Douglass had been repeatedly thrown to the ground. It was where he slept for much of the first two decades of his life, and it was to the ground his body was forced when he was beaten, not just by Covey, but by others as well. Naturally, he wished no more of that kind of humble existence. In his first twenty years, he had more than enough humiliations for a lifetime. Still, Frederick displayed humility in the face of humiliations through his cultivation of a quiet dignity that soon would roar. Without this, he could have despaired and taken his own life or allowed his spirit to be quenched. Instead, he held his own and adhered to a constant view of who he was and who he might become. He was honest about himself and his own nature, and he recognized that despite the humiliations he suffered, he still needed to be a decent man. He was more than decent, in fact, and steeled his soul so that it would not be given over to the same tyranny that was everywhere around him. This attitude of humility in the midst of humiliation allowed him eventually to gain the pride that was worth more than all the wealth of the world.

Douglass's existence under Covey was not unlike the later experience of prisoners in Communism's "gulag archipelago," as the great Russian writer Aleksandr Solzhenitsyn called the Soviet system of concentration camps and prisons.[32] The American system of slavery shared with the later ideology of Communism an ironclad commitment to stamping out in the human soul any real hope for liberty. A slave, just like a Russian *zek*, or "prisoner," must never be given by his breaker, master, or owner any inkling of hope, lest it render him unfit for his existence as a slave. What Douglass called "the systematic tyranny of slavery" made him at times doubt the providence of God, as it would many others held in Soviet captivity a century later.[33] During his enslavement, Douglass found his "mind passing over the whole scale or circle of belief and unbelief, from faith in the over-ruling Providence of God, to the blackest atheism."[34] Despite his doubts, Douglass's enduring faith in God helped him bear up under the pressures of his captivity. In this aspect of tyranny, too, the experience of many under Communism's iron grip, including Solzhenitsyn himself, was like that of the American slave.

Communism denied the existence of God, while slave interests used his existence for the ideological purpose of propping up a regime of inequality. Slavery said some human beings were so imperfect they could be property, while Communism claimed that all human beings, subjected to the right conditions, could be made perfect. The Confederacy promised the dawn of a new day for those who believed that slavery, in the words of its vice president, Alexander Stephens, should be the "cornerstone" of the regime.[35] Communism promised the creation of a "new Soviet man," an act that would usher in a new era of prosperity and peace. In holding out the possibility of these new things, both ideologies—slavery and Communism—relied upon brutal force to keep their subjects from rising up. Each struggled to subdue its populace, however, when those enslaved retained what Solzhenitsyn called "a point of view."[36]

A point of leverage that allows for spiritual resistance to

tyranny, the "point of view" is held by a person who refuses internally to submit to an ideological lie. For those held in slavery, the lie they were told was that they were worthless except insofar as they served their masters. For those held captive by Communism, the lie they were told was that they were worthless except insofar as they served the global revolutionary cause. In both cases, a person could submit internally and then outwardly accept the lie, or resist internally and live by the truth. Resistance sometimes had an outward manifestation, as in efforts, whether peaceful or violent, to escape subjugation. Whatever the outward manifestation, resistance, Solzhenitsyn claimed, requires an interior rejection of untruth.[37] This interior stance is what Solzhenitsyn calls a "point of view," or what one "treasures more than life itself." As Gleb Nerzhin, the main character in Solzhenitsyn's novel *In the First Circle*, discovers in his journey, which is based in large part on the Russian writer's own experience in prison, it is "one's soul" that matters most. "And each of us fashions his soul himself, year in and year out. You must strive to temper and to cut and polish your soul so as to become a human being."[38] When subjected to abuse or even torture—spiritual, mental, or physical—a person with a point of view feels no less pain than another. But however much that person might suffer, he does not put survival above all else. He is not afraid to die. In retaining a principled opposition to oppression, a person with a point of view gains hope. Even if the outward subjugation continues, an inner peace prevails.

Frederick Douglass "polished" his soul even as a young man. In so doing he gained a point of view whose power, by the time he was sixteen years old, would be witnessed first by Edward Covey and then the world. For much of his youth, Douglass believed that for him and other slaves, "God required them to submit to slavery and to wear their chains with meekness and humility."[39] Having believed that resistance by a slave against his master, especially when violent, was wrong, Douglass discovered that his introduction to learning led him to question that position. His experience under Covey further undermined it, and one incident exploded it altogether.

Covey loved to lie in wait for Douglass, so that when the boy least suspected his presence Covey would leap out and beat him. Having endured many such attacks, in addition to all the other beatings, Douglass decided that he had endured enough and at the next opportunity would resist his master. When Covey launched yet another sneak attack on him, this time in the horse stable, Douglass decided that he would act on his newfound resolve and resist with all his might the man who sought to break him. In an instant Douglass found himself in an epic struggle. *"Are you going to resist, you scoundrel?"* Covey asked Frederick, to which he responded, *"Yes, sir."* Having put Covey and his cousin, whom Covey had called in for backup, on the defensive, Frederick repeated his intention to "resist."[40] When Covey could not coerce his hired hands or other slaves into helping him subdue Frederick, he knew he was in trouble. Frederick could have gone on the offensive and left Covey hurting, but his complete success in what was purely a defensive effort had its intended effect: Covey never touched him again.

In this monumental act of resistance, Douglass accomplished what he later understood as "the turning-point" in his existence as a slave. "Human nature is so constituted," he wrote after the incident, "that it cannot *honor* a helpless man, though it can *pity* him, and even this it cannot do long if signs of power do not rise." Having shown himself that he could be powerful in self-protection, Frederick testified, "This spirit made me a freeman in *fact*, though I still remained a slave in *form*." Douglass displayed an interior resistance to slavery that, although it was not immediately rewarded with freedom, bestowed upon him a feeling of "independence" unlike anything else he had ever experienced.[41]

"NOW A WEASEL, NOW A WHALE, NOW NOTHING"

Douglass served out the remaining half of his year on Covey's farm, and after several failed efforts at running away not long after that, he succeeded in escaping. Upon doing so, he felt an elation he had not experienced before that time. "A new world had opened upon me.... I lived more in one day than in a year of my slave life."[42]

Before ending up in New Bedford, Massachusetts, where he assumed the surname Douglass, the newly free man also became a married man, wedding Anna Murray, the daughter of slaves, in New York in 1838. The young couple's search for a church in Massachusetts was a reminder that while they were free, they were far from equal. The black people in one church they visited, typical of most, "looked like sheep without a shepherd." Their "bearing," Douglass said, "was most humiliating."[43] Only after the whites were served Communion did the presiding clergyman invite the black members of the church—Douglass observed that they looked like "black sheep" who had been "penned" in the corner—to partake in the sacrament. For Douglass, the preening self-righteousness of the whole display, combined with the obvious absurdity perpetuated by segregating a feast meant to enshrine the equality of all believers before God, was more than he could bear. They departed that church, never again to return. Instead, they joined another church, the African Methodist Episcopal Zion Church, whose services did not remind him of his life as a slave.

Later, licensed to preach by his church and eager to take the opportunity to speak publicly whenever he could, Douglass developed a reputation as an excellent orator. His remarkable story and impressive manner of telling it so moved the abolitionist William Lloyd Garrison that upon first hearing Douglass speak in April 1841, the well-known and charismatic leader of the abolitionist movement in America responded with a strong endorsement of the young ex-slave. Countless others were similarly moved by Douglass's compelling story. He was so eloquent, in fact, that some thought it impossible that he could have been enslaved, a contention Douglass was able to quickly refute by showing any doubters the scars on his back. He was "a graduate from the peculiar institution, *with [his] diploma written on his back.*"[44]

As Douglass launched what was to become a brilliant career as a leading orator and journalistic crusader for the abolition of slavery, he came under the early influence of Garrison and, in turn, the anti-Constitutionalism of the Garrisonian school of thought. As the founding editor of abolitionism's leading newspaper, the *Liberator,* for thirty-five years, Garrison exercised enormous sway over the movement as a whole. Garrison was a committed Protestant, and his religious ardor was outdone only by his devotion to the purity of the cause of abolition. Believing the Constitution "the most bloody and heaven-daring arrangement ever made by men" for the protection of slavery, Garrison rejected it, along with what he saw as any other political compromise with slavery.[45] Politics was the realm into which morality went to be corrupted, Garrison held. Nothing pure could come of politics, and so no one seeking purity should be involved in it. So strong was his antipolitical ire for most of his career that one might say he was as much against politics as he was against slavery. In this stance, Garrison's example at first proved convincing to Douglass.

Drawn to Garrison because of his ideological purity on some of the most controversial issues facing abolitionists, including the question of whether blacks should be colonized to Africa (Garrison was against this), Douglass was more strident than Garrison in his feeling of betrayal by the early American policies on slavery. "I have no love for America, as such; I have no patriotism," Douglass proclaimed. "I have no country. What country have I? . . . I have not, I cannot have, any love for this country, as such, or for its Constitution. I desire to see its overthrow as speedily as possible, and its Constitution shivered in a thousand fragments."[46] From a man who loved the words of the Declaration of Independence, a hatred of the Constitution seemed incongruous, but what Douglass felt deeply was that the Declaration's promise of equality was betrayed when the Constitution's creation sanctioned slavery. Like Garrison, Douglass could not understand how the principles of the Declaration could have been compromised away so quickly in the Constitution. By allowing slavery, both men felt, the Founding Fathers of the nation gave up any claim they had to justice. Only an appeal to heaven, not the grimy art of politics, could rescue the republic. This was Douglass's main message throughout the 1840s, given wide reading in his own newspaper, the *North Star*, which he founded in 1847.

On May 23, 1851, in an article titled "Change of Opinion Announced," Frederick Douglass stated that after two years of soul-searching, he now believed that the Constitution was an antislavery document. His volte-face brought next-day denouncements from Garrison and other hard-line abolitionists, but Douglass did not care, for his discovery of the possibility of healthy political compromise came along with an embrace of his country as he never before felt. As a symbolic gesture of his newfound patriotism, Douglass used the salutation "Fellow Citizens" to greet the audiences to whom he spoke, which continued to grow nationwide. Rather than eschewing political activity as inherently evil, Douglass embraced the give-and-take of politics. In coming to see human beings as social and political creatures, he realized that political compromise was not the worst of all evils.

To understand the Constitution, Douglass found, one had to read it in light of its original meaning, not that imposed by later generations who made up their minds without sufficient examination of the evidence. "What, then, is the Constitution?" he asked in an 1860 speech. His answer was a reflection on constitutional construction: "It is no vague, indefinite, floating, unsubstantial, ideal something, colored according to any man's fancy, now a weasel, now a whale, and now nothing."[47] Douglass came to see the Constitution as worth defending because a careful reading of its clauses concerning slavery revealed that they were like the scaffolding of a "magnificent structure" that is able "to be removed as soon as the building was completed."[48] Douglass noted that the framers of the Constitution intentionally did not write into their "glorious freedom document" any explicit mention of slavery. They used artful or even clever euphemisms, but rather than construe that usage as hypocritical, Douglass urged its readers to consider the intention of the drafters. As James Madison said of those efforts, they did not want to give slavery "moral" standing by legal recognition of it by name.[49] (Compare the U.S. Constitution to the Confederate one, Douglass might have added, which pronounced the legality of slavery proudly and without any moral compunction.)

Douglass had other, specific rejoinders to those who claimed of the four especially troublesome clauses of the Constitution that they indicted not only the Founders but the document itself, and each amounted to a plea for a reading that took into account the plain meaning of each clause, as well as the debate that produced it, in addition to the larger, noble purposes for which the document was created in the first place.

Douglass's new mode of constitutional thinking renewed his love of first principles. In becoming more open to the truth of the Constitution's meaning and investigating claims that earlier he had taken for granted, Douglass grew in his willingness to change. He had always thought he was repairing to foundational principles, but in dogmatically clinging to Garrisonianism, Douglass had not taken the time to do his own inquiry. The truths of the Declaration took on even greater meaning for him as he discovered a new way of understanding the Constitution. In urging a humility before the natural law and natural rights principles of the Declaration and Constitution, Douglass helped to instill in Americans a pride in who they were as a people and also who they could become.

Douglass's conversion to a new understanding of America, however, did not mean that he became a blind defender of everything the Founders did, much less the political leadership of the day. A frequent critic of both abolitionists and those in political power, Douglass was a more effective reformer after his turn from Garrison. Reform implies the existence of a form, and the form of the American republic was and is the principles of the Declaration *and* the Constitution, devotion to which Douglass pledged with all of his heart. Renouncing the tension that he had alleged to exist between the Declaration and the Constitution, Douglass became a powerful force for moving America to better realize the goals of both documents.

"TRUTH WAS POWERFUL"

Douglass spent the decade before the Civil War, the four years of the war itself, and the decades thereafter doing much the same thing: pleading on behalf of firm action in ending slavery, preserving the Union, and winning lasting liberty for former slaves. The only man to speak on behalf of female suffrage at the 1848 Seneca Falls conference in New York, Douglass was a defender of many causes, all of which had the common mission of helping those who lacked a voice. Looking back on his life of fighting injustice, Douglass was especially proud that when his friend Elizabeth Cady Stanton had stood at Seneca Falls to propose that women be granted the vote, Douglass seconded the motion. "When I ran away from slavery," he said in 1888, at the International Council of Women, forty years after

Seneca Falls, "it was for myself; when I advocated emancipation, it was for my people; but when I stood up for the rights of woman, self was out of the question, and I found a little nobility in the act."[50]

Earning his living as an orator in addition to his newspaper editorial duties, Douglass delivered a consistent message about man's potential and the purpose of government. These topics and more he covered in a speech "The Self-Made Man," one that he delivered more than fifty times around the country. In this popular talk, he underscored his care for those who begin life on the lowest rung of the ladder. "It is natural to revolt at squalor," he said, "but we may well relax our lip of scorn and contempt when we stand among the lowly and despised, for out of the rags of the meanest cradle there may come a great man and this is a treasure richer than all the wealth of the Orient."[51] America offers opportunity for greatness unlike any other land. "In Europe, greatness is often thrust upon men. They are made legislators by birth." Extolling hard work and downplaying the role of luck or fortune in life, Douglass recognized that, as was the case in his own story, much can come from little: "From apparently the basest metals we have the finest toned bells, and we are taught respect from simple manhood when we see how, from the various dregs of society, there come men who may well be regarded as the pride and as the watch towers of the race."[52]

Douglass made these claims mindful that even though he used the phrase the "self-made man," in the deepest sense of that expression, no such man exists. No man is an island, Douglass admitted, such that he can do it all alone, free of assistance from his fellows and those who came before him. Douglass's idea of greatness, then, was not exactly Aristotle's idea of magnanimity. Greatness of soul is what matters most, Douglass said, concurring with Aristotle. But where Douglass would differ from the ancient thinker is in saying that greatness is consistent with wonder before the divine. Whereas Aristotle left little if any room in the heart of the magnanimous man for piety, Douglass demanded in his idea of greatness a spirit that says, "There but by the grace of God go I."

Douglass's humility gave rise in his soul to hope. His combination of humility and greatness of soul allowed him to push back against the hopelessness that confronted him not just in his childhood but in his later life, too, for while nothing after his twenties would compare with the degradation he suffered as a slave, he still faced plenty of challenges as a freeman. Greatest of these was the question of whether or not the citizens of the United States would change their hearts and minds and embrace black people as equal in dignity and rights to white people.

Abraham Lincoln's Emancipation Proclamation acted as a strong answer in the affirmative to that question and a balm to Douglass's soul. Speaking at Hillsdale College on January 21, 1863, three weeks after the Proclamation went into effect, Douglass called it a "fatal blow" that had "been struck at the root of the gigantic evil."[53] When slaves rose up in the South, he said, they could now do it in accord with, rather than against, the law. "It was a proud thought," he added, "that the first man to put the knife of military power to the throat of this vile monster, was an Illinoisan."[54] Paying tribute to Lincoln on that happy occasion, Douglass also recognized William Lloyd Garrison. Although Douglass had broken with his former mentor some twelve years before, the victory marked by the Proclamation, Douglass claimed, owed much to Garrison's indefatigable work. "Truth was powerful; a single individual, armed with truth, was a majority against the world," Douglass stated in honor of Garrison.[55] "We had attempted to contravene the laws of God by transforming men into beasts of burden," he concluded, but in throwing off the yoke of slavery Americans would return to the truth that brings life and liberty.[56]

As Frederick Douglass traveled all across the land, speaking, making connections along the Underground Railroad (his own home in Rochester, New York, was a stop for hundreds of slaves), and generally galvanizing activists everywhere, he had to suffer indignities that might have undone a lesser individual. Physically beaten on several occasions, routinely insulted, and harassed on more occasions than he could count, Douglass resisted the temptation, as he gained notoriety and popularity as an abolitionist orator, to turn from righteous indignation to haughty hatred. One incident, related by Booker T. Washington, captures Douglass's ability to resist this temptation. Forced into riding in the baggage car of a train in Pennsylvania, despite having paid the same fare as the white passengers, Douglass was approached by some of the white passengers, who apologized for the indignity. As Booker Washington relates it, one passenger said, "I am sorry, Mr. Douglass, that you have been degraded in this manner." To this Douglass responded, "They cannot degrade Frederick Douglass. The soul that is within me no man can degrade. I am not the one that is being degraded on account of this treatment, but those who are inflicting it upon me."[57]

Maintaining what Thomas Aquinas called the "strength of hope," Frederick Douglass displayed a personal confidence as well as a moral confidence that the rightness of his cause would win out.[58] On "his side," Douglass said, were "all the invisible forces of the moral government of the universe."[59] Aleksandr Solzhenitsyn predicted that Communism could not last and that it would be defeated in his lifetime. Douglass, who died in 1895, less than a quarter century before the Russian Revolution of 1917, upheld a moral certainty about slavery similar to that of the Russian writer who did so much to topple Communism.

Douglass's confidence that slavery would be ended was a certainty not born of arrogance but of a belief in hard work and a hope that truth will win out. After helping to end legalized slavery in the United States, Douglass worked on behalf of equality for all people. He served his country as U.S. marshal for the District of Columbia and as minister and general consul to Haiti for three years. His last day was spent with Susan B. Anthony and other leading figures of the women's suffrage movement, at a meeting in Washington, D.C., of the Women's National Council at which he had stayed late. What generations of Americans had forgotten, Frederick Douglass remembered. In his life he ennobled a nation.

PART III

AN AGE OF ARROGANCE

NINE

THE FRAGILE BRILLIANCE OF GLASS

After Rome's fall in the fifth century after Christ, Saint Augustine wrote that to live in an empire is to know only fleeting happiness: "The only joy to be attained had the fragile brilliance of glass, a joy outweighed by the fear that it may be shattered in any moment."[1] The empire of the Eternal City lasted longer than any previous Western regime had, but ultimately it met the fate of all empires. Imperial hubris, Augustine wrote, led to Rome's collapse.

As terrible as was the fall of the Roman Empire, early Americans held that the Roman republic's descent into empire was the real tragedy. The goal of America's Founders was to succeed where Rome failed—to put republican, or representative, government on such a strong foundation that it would not succumb to the threat of tyranny. Brutus and Cassius, not Julius Caesar, were more commonly the heroes of the American Founders.

For the Founders, magnanimity's claim on the Roman soul was

impressive but also cause for concern. Was it not in the service of a war-making machine? Did it not pave the way to tyranny? Virtue has to be in the service of the right purposes, the Founders held, echoing Augustine's theme, or it will not end up securing the liberty that matters most. Power for the sake of power is unsustainable. Power for the sake of glory is pride run amok. To live life in search of praise from people is empty. As Augustine said, in words that echo across the ages, "Smoke has no weight."[2]

"TO DOUBT A LITTLE OF HIS OWN INFALLIBILITY"

In his project for moral improvement, Benjamin Franklin's little book of virtues filled up quickly with marks reminding him of his faults and failures. Humility was an especially hard virtue for him, and its mastery always eluded him. It would elude anyone, he concluded, for just as soon as someone thinks himself perfectly humble, he is likely to succumb to the temptation of pride. Franklin's dilemma—America's dilemma at our founding—was how to be humble and achieve greatness. Our challenge today is how to rediscover humility.

At the Constitutional Convention of Philadelphia, Franklin was regarded by the other delegates as the elder statesman. It was fitting, then, that the meeting's last word went to him. Thirty-seven others joined Franklin in signing the Constitution on September 17, 1787 (one delegate affixed two signatures, one for himself and the other on behalf of an ailing, absent member of Delaware's delegation). As the signers strode to the front of the room, the eighty-one-year-old

Franklin reflected on the painting of a sun that was on the back of the president's chair. Throughout the long and difficult deliberations, Franklin wondered whether the sun depicted was setting or rising. "But now at length," he concluded, "I have the happiness to know that it is a rising and not a setting sun."[3]

Some Americans are familiar with that story, but few know that the preceding speech Franklin made at the Convention, that same day, harkened back to the project for moral improvement he had embarked upon more than half a century before in an indirect but profound way. Right after the Constitution was read aloud for all of the delegates, Franklin had his fellow Pennsylvanian James Wilson read his prepared remarks. Invoking his long experience in life, Franklin indicated that he had often changed his opinion, "even on important subjects." There were parts of the Constitution with which he disagreed, but he planned to vote for the new frame of government, he said, and urged everyone to do likewise. Infallibility is not man's domain: "For when you assemble a number of men to have the advantage of their joint wisdom, you inevitably assemble with those men, all their prejudices, their passions, their errors of opinion, their local interests, and their selfish views. From such an assembly can a perfect production be expected?"[4] Even though the Constitution was not perfect, it is astonishingly close to it, he stated. "The opinions I have had of its errors," Franklin offered, "I sacrifice to the public good." Closing with an appeal for a unanimous vote in approval of the Constitution, Franklin asked everyone "to doubt a little of his own infallibility."[5]

As part of his autobiographical reflections on his project for moral improvement, Franklin related a tale about a man and his ax.

Wanting the whole of it to be as bright as the blade, the man agreed to turn the wheel of the ax sharpener owned by his blacksmith friend if the smith would wield the blade. The wheel-turning was hard work, and eventually seeing that his ax had only turned speckled and was not yet perfect, the man told his friend he was finished—that he liked "a speckled ax best."[6] Franklin went on to state that if a man makes moral perfection his goal at the expense of friendships or other facets of a well-balanced life, he will do injustice to himself and those around him. That conclusion might have spelled the end of his project, but Franklin did not take away that lesson in his own life. He did not settle for the speckled ax. Even when his struggle to become humble proved as hard as it did, he wrote of that quest with approval, concluding that in more than fifty years it had made his life better and his relationships with others stronger.

There is no twelve- or thirteen-step program to master humility. There is no formula for becoming humble. This is true for individuals as well as nations. George Washington's humility, as great as it was, cannot substitute for ours today. We cannot hold off on the hard work of humility, praying that a modern-day Washington, Madison, Adams, Lincoln, or Douglass will do it for us. Humility is a quality of the soul that cannot be perfected but can be practiced. America is not Rome—yet. There is no guarantee of national greatness. The arrogance of our age supposes that prosperity is perpetual and success inevitable. America's history of hard-won humility tells us otherwise. As individuals and as a people, we must rediscover our greatest virtue.

NOTES

Chapter 1: Benjamin Franklin's Dilemma

1. Edward Gibbon, *The History of the Decline and Fall of the Roman Empire*, vol. 2, ed. David Womersley (New York: Penguin, 1994), 509.

2. Muhammad Ali, as quoted in Arlene Schulman and Martha Cosgrove, *Muhammad Ali* (Minneapolis: Lerner Publishing Group, 2005), 47.

3. Augustine, "Letter 118," in *Letters 1–155*, trans. Roland Teske, part 2, vol. 2 of *The Works of Saint Augustine: A Translation for the 21st Century*, ed. Boniface Ramsey (Hyde Park, NY: New City Press, 2003), 116–17. Augustine's Latin word for pride, *superbia*, connotes arrogance, not the healthy kind of pride.

4. Saint Bernard of Clairvaux, as quoted in Peter Kreeft, *Back to Virtue* (San Francisco: Ignatius Press, 1992), 99.

5. Benjamin Franklin, *Autobiography*, in *Writings*, ed. J. A. Leo Lemay (New York: Library of America, 1987), 1383.

6. Ibid., 1392.

7. Ibid., 1385.

8. Ibid.

9. Ibid., 1387.

10. Ibid., 1393.

11. Ibid.

12. Ibid.

13. Thomas Aquinas, *Summa Theologiae*, II–II, Qu. 161, Art. 2, ad. 3, trans. T. C. O'Brien (London: Blackfriars, 1964), 97.

14. Augustine, *City of God*, trans. Henry Bettenson (New York: Penguin, 1984), 5 (I.Preface).

Chapter 2: Jesus and Socrates

1. John Cotton, *The New England Primer* (Glasgow: John and William Shaw, 1781), 14.
2. Augustine, *City of God*, 571 (XIV.12).
3. Ibid., 569 (XIV.11).
4. Ibid., 572 (XIV.13).
5. Ibid.
6. *Merriam-Webster's Collegiate Dictionary*, 11th ed., s.v. "humble."
7. Homer, *Iliad*, bk. 2, trans. Richmond Lattimore (Chicago: University of Chicago Press, 1951), 82.
8. Ibid.
9. Ibid., bk. 1, 59.
10. Plato, *Apology of Socrates*, in Thomas G. West and Grace Starry West, trans., *Four Texts on Socrates, Plato and Aristophanes: Plato's "Euthyphro," "Apology," "Crito" and Aristophanes' "Clouds,"* rev. ed. (Ithaca, NY: Cornell University Press, 1998), 82 (29a).
11. Thomas G. West, introduction, in West, *Four Texts on Socrates*, 20.
12. Plato, *Apology of Socrates*, in West, *Four Texts on Socrates*, 80 (30e).
13. Aristotle, *Nicomachean Ethics*, trans. J. A. K. Thomson (New York: Penguin, 1976), 155 (IV, 1123b35).
14. Ibid., 156 (IV, 1124b1).
15. Winston Churchill, quoted in Carl Eric Bechhofer Roberts, *Winston Churchill, being an account of the life of the Right Hon. Winston Leonard Spencer Churchill, P.C., C.H., T.D., M.P.* (London: Mills and Boon, 1927), 102.
16. Aristotle, *Nicomachean Ethics*, 157 (IV, 1124b20).
17. Ibid., 157 (IV, 1124b23).
18. Ibid., 158 (IV, 1125a9).
19. Ibid., 158 (IV, 1125a11).
20. Augustine, "Sermon 70A," in *Sermons*, trans. Edmund Hill, vol. 3 of *The Works of Saint Augustine: A Translation for the 21st Century*, ed. John E. Rotelle (Hyde Park, NY: New City Press, 2003, 1990–1997), 244.

Chapter 3: The City of the Humble and the City of the Proud

1. Augustine, *Confessions*, trans. Henry Chadwick (New York: Oxford University Press, 1991), 155 (ii.2).
2. Ibid., 52 (i.1).

3. Ibid., 159 (iv.7).
4. Ibid., 47 (viii.16).
5. Ibid., 52 (i.1).
6. Augustine, *City of God*, trans. Henry Bettenson (New York: Penguin, 1984), 42 (I.30).
7. Ibid., 220 (V.24).
8. Ibid.
9. Ibid., 219–20 (V.24).
10. Karl Löwith, "Can There Be a Christian Gentleman?" *Theology Today* 5:1 (April 1948): 63.
11. Aristotle, *Nicomachean Ethics*, trans. J. A. K. Thomson (New York: Penguin, 1976), 153 (IV, 1123b1).
12. Aquinas, *Summa Theologiae*, II–II, Q. 161, Art. 1, ad. 2, trans. T. C. O'Brien (London: Blackfriars, 1964), 93.
13. Ibid., Q. 161, Art. 2, ad. 2, 95.
14. Niccoló Machiavelli, *The Prince*, trans. Harvey C. Mansfield Jr. (Chicago: University of Chicago Press, 1985), 61 (XV).
15. Ibid., 69 (XVIII).
16. Ibid., 61 (XV).
17. Ibid., 70 (XVIII).
18. Ibid., 23 (VI).
19. Quoted in Thomas Hobbes, *Leviathan*, trans. and ed. Edwin Curley (Indianapolis: Hackett, 1994), 210 (I.xxviii.27). Hobbes is quoting Job 41:33–34.
20. Hobbes, *Leviathan*, 458 (III.xlvi.13).
21. Ibid., 109 (II.xvii.13).
22. Alexander Hamilton, "The Farmer Refuted," February 23, 1775, in *The U.S. Constitution: A Reader* (Hillsdale, MI: Hillsdale College Press, 2012), 95–96. All selections from *The U.S. Constitution: A Reader* are available at www.constitutionreader.com

Chapter 4: George Washington

1. Douglas A. McIntyre and Michael B. Sauter, "The Net Worth of the U.S. Presidents: Washington to Obama," *Atlantic*, May 20, 2010, http://www.theatlantic.com/business/archive/2010/05/the-net -worth-of-the-us-presidents-from-washington-to-obama/57020/#.

2. Quoted in David Hackett Fischer, *Washington's Crossing* (Oxford: Oxford University Press, 2004), 428.

3. Douglas Southall Freeman, *George Washington*, abridged version (New York: Touchstone, 1968), 574.

4. John Ferling, *The Ascent of George Washington: The Hidden Political Genius of an American Icon* (New York: Bloomsbury Press, 2009), 368.

5. Ron Chernow, *Washington: A Life* (New York: Penguin, 2010), 27.

6. George Washington, "Rules of Civility," in William B. Allen, ed., *George Washington: A Collection* (Indianapolis: Liberty Fund, 1988), 9.

7. Ibid., 8.

8. Ibid., 13.

9. Montesquieu, quoted in Lorraine Smith Pangle and Thomas L. Pangle, *The Learning of Liberty: The Educational Ideas of the American Founders* (Lawrence: University Press of Kansas, 1993), 242.

10. Douglass Adair, "Fame and the Founding Fathers," in Trevor Colbourn, ed., *Fame and the Founding Fathers: Essays* (Indianapolis: Liberty Fund, 1974), 16.

11. Alexander Hamilton, *Federalist* 72, in *The U.S. Constitution: A Reader*, 358.

12. George Washington, quoted in Tony Williams, *America's Beginnings: The Dramatic Events That Shaped a Nation's Character* (New York: Rowman and Littlefield, 2010), 65.

13. Chernow, *Washington*, 69.

14. Abigail Adams, quoted in Richard Brookhiser, *Founding Father: Rediscovering George Washington* (New York: Free Press, 1996), 115.

15. Glenn A. Phelps, *George Washington and American Constitutionalism* (Lawrence: University Press of Kansas, 1993), 38.

16. Ibid., 40.

17. George Washington, "Letter to Henry Laurens," December 22, 1777, in Philander D. Chase, ed., *The Papers of George Washington: Revolutionary War Series*, vol. 7 (Charlottesville: University Press of Virginia, 1996), 669.

18. Quoted in Norman Gelb, "Winter of Discontent," *Smithsonian*, May 2003, 66.

19. Ibid., 68.

20. Washington, "To Colonel Lewis Nicola," May 22, 1782, in Allen, ed., *George Washington: A Collection*, 203–4.

21. Washington, "Circular to the States," June 24, 1783, in Allen, ed., *George Washington: A Collection*, 242.

22. Ibid., 246.

23. Ibid., 249.

24. Quoted in Gordon Wood, *The Radicalism of the American Revolution* (New York: A. A. Knopf, 1992), 208.

25. Washington, "Address to Congress on Resigning His Commission," December 23, 1783, in Allen, ed., *George Washington: A Collection*, 272.

26. Ibid., 273.

27. Washington, "To the Ministers, Elders, Deacons, and Members of the Reformed German Congregation of New York," November 27, 1783, in Allen, ed., *George Washington: A Collection*, 270.

28. Ibid.

29. "Eleanor Parke Custis Lewis to Jared Sparks, 26 February 1833," in Jared Sparks, ed., *The Writings of George Washington*, vol. 12 (Boston: American Stationers' Company, 1837), 407.

30. Washington, "Circular to the States," June 14, 1783, in Allen, ed., *George Washington: A Collection*, 239.

31. Washington, "Address to Congress on Resigning His Commission," December 23, 1783, in Allen, ed., *George Washington: A Collection*, 273.

32. Stanley Weintraub, *General Washington's Christmas Farewell: A Mount Vernon Homecoming, 1783* (New York: Free Press, 2007), 163.

33. Richard Beeman, *Plain, Honest Men: The Making of the American Constitution* (New York: Random House, 2009), 30.

34. George Washington, marginalia in *Acts of the First Congress, 1789*, Collection of Mount Vernon Estate, Mount Vernon, VA.

35. George Washington, letter to Jacob Morris, May 29, 1787. From original letter, unchronicled elsewhere, Liberty Hall Museum Manuscript Collection, Kean University, Union, New Jersey. Transcription of letter provided by Terry Golway, director, Liberty Hall Collection at Kean University.

36. James Madison, *Notes of Debates in the Federal Convention of 1787* (New York: W. W. Norton, 1987), 655.

37. Washington, "Letter to Alexander Hamilton," August 28, 1788, in Allen, ed., *George Washington: A Collection*, 417.

38. Washington, "Letter to the United Baptist Churches in Virginia," May 10, 1789, in Allen, ed., *George Washington: A Collection*, 532.

39. "Moses Seixas et al. to George Washington," in W. W. Abbot et al., eds., *The Papers of George Washington: Presidential Series*, vol. 6 (Charlottesville: University Press of Virginia, 1996), 284–86.

40. Washington, "Letter to the Hebrew Congregation, Newport, Rhode Island," in Allen, ed., *George Washington: A Collection*, 548. Washington quotes Micah 4:4.

41. Washington, "Rules of Civility," in Allen, ed., *George Washington: A Collection*, 13.

42. Washington, "Farewell Address," in Allen, ed., *George Washington: A Collection*, 147.

43. Washington, "Thanksgiving Proclamation," October 3, 1789, in Allen, ed., *George Washington: A Collection*, 535.

44. Washington, "Circular to the States," June 14, 1783, in Allen, ed., *George Washington: A Collection*, 249.

45. George Washington to Colonel Benedict Arnold, September 14, 1775, in W. W. Abbot, et al., eds., *The Papers of George Washington: Revolutionary War Series*, vol. 1 (Charlottesville: University Press of Virginia, 1985), 455–56.

46. Washington to the Pennsylvania Legislature, September 12, 1789, in Abbot, ed., *The Papers of George Washington: Presidential Series*, vol. 4, 24.

47. Thomas Aquinas, *Summa Theologiae*, II–II, Qu. 161, Art. 2, ad. 3, trans. T. C. O'Brien (London: Blackfriars, 1964), 97.

48. Washington, "Rules of Civility," in Allen, ed., *George Washington: A Collection*, 13.

49. Henry Holcombe, "A Sermon Occasioned by the Death of Washington," in Ellis Sandoz, ed., *Political Sermons of the Founding Era, 1730–1805* (Indianapolis: Liberty Fund, 1991), 1408.

Chapter 5: James Madison

1. James Madison to Thomas Jefferson, quoted in Richard Beeman, *Plain, Honest Men: The Making of the American Constitution* (New York: Random House, 2009), 41.

2. George Washington to Arthur Lee, May 20, 1787, quoted in Richard Brookhiser, *Founding Father: Rediscovering George Washington* (New York: Free Press, 1996), 57.

3. Harrison Gray Otis, quoted in Ralph Ketcham, *James Madison: A Biography* (Newtown, CT: American Political Biography Press, 1971), 597.

4. William L. Smith to Edward Rutledge, August 9, 1789, quoted in John P. Kaminski, ed., *The Founders on the Founders: Word Portraits from the American Revolutionary Era* (Charlottesville: University of Virginia Press, 2008), 379.

5. Fisher Ames, "To George Richards Minot," May 18, 1789, in W. B. Allen, ed., *Works of Fisher Ames* (Indianapolis: Liberty Fund, 1983), 628.

6. William Constable to Gouverneur Morris, July 29, 1789, quoted in Kaminski, ed., *The Founders on the Founders*, 379.

7. John Randolph, March 19, 1806, memoranda by William Plumer, quoted in Kaminski, ed., *The Founders on the Founders*, 385.

8. Aristotle, *Nicomachean Ethics*, trans. J. A. K. Thomson (New York: Penguin, 1976), 158 (1125a23).

9. Thomas Hobbes, *Leviathan*, trans. and ed. Edwin Curley (Indianapolis: Hackett, 1994), 60 (I.xi.14).

10. John Witherspoon, quoted in Ketcham, *James Madison: A Biography*, 38.

11. Ibid., 39.

12. Woodrow Wilson, "Princeton in the Nation's Service: An Oration Delivered at the Princeton Sesquicentennial Celebration, Oct. 21, 1896," *The Forum* XXII (December 1896), 452.

13. John Witherspoon, quoted in Ketcham, *James Madison: A Biography*, 47.

14. Ketcham, *James Madison: A Biography*, 46.

15. John Witherspoon, "Christian Magnanimity," in *The Selected Writings of John Witherspoon*, ed. Thomas Miller (Carbondale: Southern Illinois University Press, 1990), 117–18.

16. Ibid., 125.

17. "The Declaration of Independence," in *The U.S. Constitution: A Reader*, 5.

18. James Madison to William Bradford, November 9, 1772, in Robert A. Rutland et al., eds., *The Papers of James Madison*, vol. 1 (Chicago: University of Chicago Press, 1973), 74.

19. Jack N. Rakove, "Politics as a Vocation," in *James Madison and the*

Creation of the American Republic, 3rd ed. (New York: Library of American Biography, 2007), 9–20.

20. George Mason, "Virginia Declaration of Rights," in Robert A. Rutland, ed., *The Papers of George Mason*, vol. 1 (Chapel Hill: University of North Carolina Press, 1970), 278.

21. "Virginia Declaration of Rights," in *The U. S. Constitution: A Reader*, 117.

22. Madison, *Federalist 55*, in *The U. S. Constitution: A Reader*, 320.

23. Madison, *Federalist 10*, in *The U. S. Constitution: A Reader*, 233.

24. Madison, *Federalist 51*, in *The U.S. Constitution: A Reader*, 288.

25. Ibid.

26. Ibid.

27. Richard K. Matthews, *If Men Were Angels: James Madison and the Heartless Empire of Reason* (Lawrence: University Press of Kansas, 1994), 22.

28. James Madison, *Federalist 57*, in Alexander Hamilton, James Madison, and John Jay, *The Federalist Papers*, ed. Clinton Rossiter (New York: Mentor, 1999), 348.

29. Madison, *Federalist 55*, in *The U.S. Constitution: A Reader*, 323.

30. Thomas Jefferson, "Virginia Statute for Religious Freedom," in *The U.S. Constitution: A Reader*, 135.

31. Thomas Jefferson to James Madison, December 8, 1784, in Rutland et al., eds., *The Papers of James Madison*, vol. 8, 178.

32. Madison, "Memorial and Remonstrance Against Religious Assessments," in *The U.S. Constitution: A Reader*, 130.

33. Ibid.

34. "The Declaration of Independence," in *The U.S. Constitution: A Reader*, 5.

35. Madison, "Property," in *The U.S. Constitution: A Reader*, 155.

36. Ibid., 156.

37. Madison, "Memorial and Remonstrance Against Religious Assessments," in *The U.S. Constitution: A Reader*, 131.

38. Thomas Jefferson, "Autobiography," in Merrill D. Peterson, *Thomas Jefferson: Writings* (New York: Library of America, 1984), 40.

39. James Madison to Thomas Jefferson, January 22, 1786, in Rutland et al., eds., *The Papers of James Madison*, vol. 8, 474.

40. Quoted in William Cabell Rives, *History of the Life and Times of James Madison*, vol. 2 (Boston: Little, Brown, and Company, 1866), 612.

41. "The Articles of Confederation," in *The U.S. Constitution: A Reader*, 164.

42. James Madison, "Vices of the Political System of the United States," in *The U.S. Constitution: A Reader*, 197–203.

43. George Washington, "Letter to John Jay," in *The U.S. Constitution: A Reader*, 183–84.

44. James Madison, *Notes of Debates in the Federal Convention of 1787* (New York: W. W. Norton, 1987), 31. See the sixth resolution of the Virginia Plan.

45. Forrest McDonald, *Novus Ordo Seclorum: The Intellectual Origins of the Constitution* (Lawrence: University Press of Kansas, 1985), 208–9.

46. Thomas Jefferson, "Autobiography," in Peterson, *Thomas Jefferson: Writings*, 40.

47. James Madison to William Cogswell, March 10, 1834, in *The Writings of James Madison*, vol. 9, ed. Gaillard Hunt (New York: Knickerbocker Press, 1910), 533.

48. James Madison, "Speech in the Virginia Ratifying Convention on the Judicial Power," June 20, 1788, in Jack N. Rakove, ed., *James Madison: Writings* (New York: Penguin, 1999), 398.

49. Madison, *Federalist* 37, in Alexander Hamilton, James Madison, and John Jay, *The Federalist Papers*, ed. Clinton Rossiter, 226.

50. Amendment I, U.S. Constitution, in *The U.S. Constitution: A Reader*, 58.

51. Madison, "Charters," January 18, 1792, in Rutland et al., eds., *The Papers of James Madison*, vol. 14, 192.

Chapter 6: Abigail Adams

1. Abigail Adams to John Adams, July 16, 1775, in Lyman H. Butterfield et al., eds., in *Adams Family Correspondence*, vol. 1 (Cambridge, MA: Harvard University Press, 1963), 246.

2. Abigail Adams to Mary Cranch, December 22, 1799, in John P. Kaminski, ed., *The Founders on the Founders: Word Portraits from the American Revolutionary Era* (Charlottesville: University of Virginia Press, 2008), 511.

3. Stephen J. Kurtz, "John Adams," in Robert A. Rutland, ed., *James Madison and the American Nation, 1751–1836: An Encyclopedia* (New York: Simon and Schuster, 1994), 2.

4. James Bayard to Alexander Hamilton, August 18, 1800, in Kaminski, ed., *The Founders on the Founders*, 54.

5. John Adams to Abigail Smith, September 30, 1764, in Butterfield et al., eds., *Adams Family Correspondence*, vol. 1, 49.

6. Abigail Smith to John Adams, October 4, 1764, in Butterfield et al., eds., *Adams Family Correspondence*, vol. 1, 50.

7. Woody Holton, *Abigail Adams* (New York: Free Press, 2009), 30.

8. Abigail Smith to Cotton Tufts, April 2, 1764, in Butterfield et al., eds., *Adams Family Correspondence*, vol. 1, 13.

9. Thomas Jefferson to James Madison, January 30, 1787, in Julian P. Boyd and Mina R. Bryan, eds., *The Papers of Thomas Jefferson*, vol. 11 (Princeton , NJ: Princeton University Press, 1955), 94.

10. John Adams, February 16, 1756, in Lyman H. Butterfield, ed., *Diary and Autobiography of John Adams* (Cambridge, MA: Harvard University Press, 1961), 7.

11. Victor Marie du Pont, quoted in Kaminski, ed., *The Founders on the Founders*, 42.

12. Thomas Paine, quoted in Kaminski, ed., *The Founders on the Founders*, 57.

13. Abigail Adams to Charles Adams, May 26, 1781, in Butterfield et al., eds., *Adams Family Correspondence*, vol. 4, 135.

14. John Adams to James Warren, December 2, 1778, in Gregg L. Lint et al., eds., *Papers of John Adams*, vol. 7 (Cambridge, MA: Harvard University Press, 1989), 244.

15. Abigail Adams to Mercy Otis Warren, December 5, 1773, in Butterfield et al., eds., *Adams Family Correspondence*, vol. 1, 88.

16. John Adams, "In Congress, Spring 1776, and Thomas Paine," in Lyman H. Butterfield, ed., *Diary and Autobiography of John Adams*, 333.

17. Fisher Ames, "To Rufus King," September 24, 1800, in W. B. Allen, ed., *Works of Fisher Ames*, vol. 2 (Indianapolis: Liberty Fund, 1983), 1385.

18. John Adams to Abigail Adams, September 26, 1775, in Butterfield et al., eds., *Adams Family Correspondence*, vol. 1, 285.

19. John Adams, September 24, 1775, in Lyman H. Butterfield, ed., *Diary and Autobiography of John Adams*, vol. 2, 182.

20. John Adams to Abigail Adams, May 27, 1776, in Butterfield et al., eds., *Adams Family Correspondence*, vol. 1, 420.

21. John Adams to Abigail Smith, February 14, 1763, in Butterfield et al., eds., *Adams Family Correspondence*, vol. 1, 3.

22. Abigail Adams to John Adams, December 30, 1773, in Butterfield et al., eds., *Adams Family Correspondence*, vol. 1, 90.

23. Abigail Adams to John Adams, July 16, 1775, in Butterfield et al., eds., *Adams Family Correspondence*, vol. 1, 246.

24. Abigail Adams to John Adams, December 15, 1783, in Richard Alan Ryerson et al., eds., *Adams Family Correspondence*, vol. 5, 280.

25. Quoted in Edith B. Gelles, *Abigail and John: Portrait of a Marriage* (New York: Harper Perennial, 2009), 119.

26. Abigail Adams to John Adams, December 15, 1783, in Ryerson et al., eds., *Adams Family Correspondence*, vol. 5, 280.

27. Abigail Adams to John Adams, March 2, 1796, in the "Adams Family Papers: An Electronic Archive," Massachusetts Historical Society, http://www.masshist.org/digitaladams/aea/cfm/doc.cfm?id=L17 960302aa.

28. Gelles, *Abigail and John: Portrait of a Marriage*, 217.

29. Abigail Adams to Isaac Smith Jr., April 20, 1771, in Butterfield et al., eds., *Adams Family Correspondence*, vol. 1, 76.

30. John Adams to Abigail Adams, July 17, 1775, in Butterfield et al., eds., *Adams Family Correspondence*, vol. 1, 241.

31. Ibid., 242.

32. Abigail Adams to John Adams, July 25, 1775, in Butterfield et al., eds., *Adams Family Correspondence*, vol. 1, 263.

33. Abigail Adams to John Adams, March 31, 1776, in Butterfield et al., eds., *Adams Family Correspondence*, vol. 1, 370.

34. Ibid., 369.

35. David McCullough, *John Adams* (New York: Simon and Schuster, 2001), 480.

36. John Adams to Abigail Adams, April 14, 1776, in Butterfield et al., eds., *Adams Family Correspondence*, vol. 1, 382.

37. Abigail Adams to John Adams, May 7, 1776, in Butterfield et al., eds., *Adams Family Correspondence*, vol. 1, 402.

38. Abigail Adams to Mercy Otis Warren, July 16, 1773, in Butterfield et al., eds., *Adams Family Correspondence*, vol. 1, 84.

39. Gelles, *Abigail and John: Portrait of a Marriage*, 38.

40. John Adams to Abigail Adams, August 3, 1776, in Butterfield et al., eds., *Adams Family Correspondence*, vol. 2, 76.

41. Abigail Adams to John Adams, August 14, 1776, in Butterfield et al., eds., *Adams Family Correspondence*, vol. 2, 94.

42. John Adams to Abigail Adams, October 29, 1775, in Butterfield et al., eds., *Adams Family Correspondence*, vol. 1, 317.

43. Abigail Adams, quoted in Holton, *Abigail Adams: A Life*, 213.

44. Abigail Adams to James Lovell, September 12, 1781, in Butterfield et al., eds., *Adams Family Correspondence*, vol. 4, 210.

45. John Adams to Abigail (Nabby) Adams, June 9, 1783, in Ryerson et al., eds., *Adams Family Correspondence*, vol. 5, 169.

Chapter 7: Abraham Lincoln

1. Abraham Lincoln, "Notes for Speeches," c. August 21, 1858, in Roy P. Basler, ed., *Collected Works of Abraham Lincoln*, vol. 2 (New Brunswick, NJ: Rutgers University Press, 1953), 548.

2. Lincoln, "Address Before the Young Men's Lyceum of Springfield, Illinois," January 27, 1838, in Basler, ed., *Collected Works*, vol. 1, 115.

3. Ibid.

4. Ibid., 112.

5. Ibid., 111.

6. Lincoln, "First Inaugural Address," March 4, 1861, in Basler, ed., *Collected Works*, vol. 4, 272.

7. Lincoln, "Address Before the Young Men's Lyceum of Springfield, Illinois," in Basler, ed., *Collected Works*, vol. 1, 113.

8. Ibid., 114.

9. Ibid.

10. Ibid., 115.

11. William H. Herndon, *Herndon's Life of Lincoln* (Rockville, MD: Wildside Press, 2008), 304.

12. Abraham Lincoln, "Reputed First Political Speech," March 1832, in T. Harry Williams, ed., *Selected Writings and Speeches of Abraham Lincoln* (New York: Hendricks House, 1943), 3.

13. Lincoln, "Letter to John T. Stuart," January 23, 1841, in Basler, ed., *Collected Works*, vol. 1, 229.

14. Allen C. Guelzo, *Abraham Lincoln: Redeemer President* (Grand Rapids, MI: William B. Eerdmans, 1999), 99.
15. Lincoln, "Letter to Joshua Speed," July 4, 1842, in Basler, ed., *Collected Works*, vol. 1, 289.
16. Lincoln, "Speech in U.S. House of Representatives on the Presidential Question," July 27, 1848, in Basler, ed., *Collected Works*, vol. 1, 509.
17. Lincoln, "Definition of Democracy," attributed to August 1, 1858, in Basler, ed., *Collected Works*, vol. 2, 532.
18. Lincoln, "First Debate with Stephen A. Douglas at Ottawa, Illinois," August 21, 1858, in Basler, ed., *Collected Works*, vol. 3, 1.
19. Lincoln, "Speech in Chicago, Illinois," July 10, 1858, in Basler, ed., *Collected Works*, vol. 2, 500.
20. Lincoln, "Speech to One Hundred Forty-Eighth Ohio Regiment," August 31, 1864, in Basler, ed., *Collected Works*, vol. 7, 528.
21. Lincoln, "Second Inaugural Address," March 4, 1865, in Basler, ed., *Collected Works*, vol. 8, 332.
22. Frederick Douglass, "Oration in Memory of Abraham Lincoln," April 14, 1876, in *Frederick Douglass: Selected Speeches and Writings*, ed. Philip S. Foner (Chicago: Lawrence Hill Books, 1999), 622.
23. George McClellan, quoted in Mackubin T. Owens, "Lincoln as Commander-in-Chief," August 2007, John M. Ashbrook Center for Public Affairs, Ashland University, http://ashbrook.org/publications/oped-owens-07-commander/. This section draws upon Owens's insights into Lincoln's leadership.
24. James McHenry, in Max Farrand, ed., *The Records of the Federal Convention*, vol. 3 (New Haven, CT: Yale University Press, 1937), 85.
25. Abraham Lincoln, quoted in Allen C. Guelzo, *Abraham Lincoln: Redeemer President*, 342.
26. Michael Burlingame, ed., "July 31, 1863," in *Inside Lincoln's White House: The Complete Civil War Diary of John Hay* (Carbondale: Southern Illinois University Press, 1999), 69.
27. Thomas Aquinas, *Summa Theologiae* I, Q. 22, Art. 2, ad. 3, trans. T. C. O'Brien (London: Blackfriars, 1964), 91.
28. Benjamin Franklin, quoted in James Madison, *Notes of Debates in the Federal Convention of 1787* (New York: W. W. Norton, 1987), 290.

29. Lincoln, "The Meditation on the Divine Will," September 30, 1862, in Basler, ed., *Collected Works*, vol. 5, 237.

30. Lincoln, "Reply to Eliza P. Gurney," October 26, 1862, in Basler, ed., *Collected Works*, vol. 5, 478.

31. Lincoln, "Address to the New Jersey Senate at Trenton, New Jersey," February 21, 1861, in Basler, ed., *Collected Works*, vol. 4, 237.

32. Abraham Lincoln, quoted in Michael Burlingame, *The Inner World of Abraham Lincoln* (Champaign: University of Illinois Press, 1997), 66.

33. Elizabeth Keckley, *Behind the Scenes, or, Thirty Years a Slave and Four Years in the White House* (1868), reprinted in Harold K. Bush, ed., *Lincoln in His Own Time* (Iowa City: University of Iowa Press, 2011), 67.

34. Michael Burlingame, ed., *With Lincoln in the White House* (Carbondale: Southern Illinois University Press, 2006), 71.

35. Allen Guelzo, *Fateful Lightning: A New History of the Civil War and Reconstruction* (New York: Oxford University Press, 2012), 214.

36. Ibid., 213.

37. Lincoln, "Reply to Eliza P. Gurney," October 26, 1862, in Basler, ed., *Collected Works*, vol. 5, 478.

38. Lincoln, "Address to the New Jersey Senate at Trenton, New Jersey," February 21, 1861, in Basler, ed., *Collected Works*, vol. 4, 237.

39. Thomas Merton, *New Seeds of Contemplation* (New York: New Directions Books, 1961), 180.

40. Lincoln, "Second Inaugural Address," March 4, 1865, in Basler, ed., *Collected Works*, vol. 8, 333.

41. Ibid.

Chapter 8: Frederick Douglass

1. Frederick Douglass, *Life and Times of Frederick Douglass*, in Frederick Douglass, *Autobiographies*, ed. Henry Louis Gates Jr. (New York: Library of America, 1994), 804.

2. Ibid., 797.

3. Frederick Douglass, "Our Work Is Not Done," December 3–4, 1863, in *Frederick Douglass: Selected Speeches and Writings*, ed. Philip S. Foner (Chicago: Lawrence Hill Books, 1999), 551.

4. Douglass, *My Bondage and My Freedom*, in *Autobiographies*, 157.

5. Douglass, *Life and Times of Frederick Douglass*, in *Autobiographies*, 484.

6. Ibid., 505.

7. Douglass, *My Bondage and My Freedom,* in *Autobiographies,* 184.

8. Douglass, *Life and Times of Frederick Douglass,* in *Autobiographies,* 510.

9. Ibid.

10. Douglass, *My Bondage and My Freedom,* in *Autobiographies,* 195.

11. Ibid., 434.

12. Frederick Douglass, "Nemesis," in *Douglass' Monthly,* May 1861, in Foner, ed., *Frederick Douglass: Selected Speeches and Writings,* 450.

13. Douglass, *Life and Times of Frederick Douglass,* in *Autobiographies,* 493.

14. Ibid., 484.

15. Ibid., 527.

16. Ibid.

17. Ibid., 532.

18. Ibid., 533.

19. Ibid., 534.

20. Ibid., 539.

21. Ibid., 559.

22. Ibid., 563.

23. Ibid., 565.

24. Ibid., 566.

25. Ibid., 572.

26. Ibid., 567.

27. Ibid., 583.

28. Ibid., 572.

29. Ibid., 574.

30. Ibid., 575.

31. Douglass, *Narrative of the Life of Frederick Douglass, An American Slave,* in *Autobiographies,* 60.

32. Aleksandr I. Solzhenitsyn, *The Gulag Archipelago, 1918–1956: An Experiment in Literary Investigation,* trans. Thomas P. Whitney, vol. 1 (New York: Westview Press, 1973), x.

33. Douglass, *Life and Times of Frederick Douglass,* in *Autobiographies,* 580.

34. Ibid., 579.

35. Alexander Stephens, "Cornerstone Speech," in *The U.S. Constitution: A Reader* (Hillsdale, MI: Hillsdale College Press, 2012), 578.

36. Aleksandr Solzhenitsyn, Letter to Fr. Sergii Zheludkov, April 28, 1972, in *Aleksandr Solzhenitsyn: Critical Essays and Documentary Materials*, ed. John B. Dunlop, Richard Haugh, and Alexis Klimoff (New York: Collier Books, 1975), 556.

37. Ibid.

38. Aleksandr I. Solzhenitsyn, *In the The First Circle*, trans. Harry T. Willetts (New York: Harper Perennial, 2009), 496.

39. Douglass, *Life and Times of Frederick Douglass*, in *Autobiographies*, 534.

40. Ibid., 588.

41. Ibid., 591.

42. Ibid., 647.

43. Douglass, *My Bondage and My Freedom*, in *Autobiographies*, 361.

44. Ibid., 365.

45. William Lloyd Garrison, "The Great [Constitutional] Crisis," in Mason Lowance, ed., *Against Slavery: An Abolitionist Reader* (New York: Penguin, 2000), 115.

46. Douglass, "The Right to Criticize American Institutions," May 11, 1847, in Foner, ed., *Frederick Douglass: Selected Speeches and Writings*, 77.

47. Douglass, "The Constitution of the United States: Is It Pro-Slavery or Antislavery?" March 26, 1860, in Foner, ed., *Frederick Douglass: Selected Speeches and Writings*, 381.

48. Douglass, "Address for the Promotion of Colored Enlistments," July 6, 1863, in Foner, ed., *Frederick Douglass: Selected Speeches and Writings*, 536.

49. The word "'legally' was struck out . . . in compliance with the wish of some who thought the term legal equivocal, and favoring the idea that slavery was legal in a moral view." James Madison, *Notes of Debates in the Federal Convention of 1787* (New York: W. W. Norton, 1987), 648.

50. Douglass, "Address before the International Council of Women," March 31, 1888, in Foner, ed., *Frederick Douglass: Selected Speeches and Writings*, 709.

51. Douglass, "Self-Made Men, An Address before the Students of the Indian Industrial School, Carlisle, Pennsylvania," Library of Congress website, http://memory.loc.gov/cgi-bin/ampage?collId=mfd&fileName=29/29002/29002page.db&recNum=1&itemLink=/ammem/doughtml/dougFolder5.html&linkText=7.

52. Ibid.

53. Frederick Douglass, "Truth and Error," in *Douglass' Monthly,*
    February 1863.

54. Ibid.

55. Ibid.

56. Ibid.

57. Booker T. Washington, *Up from Slavery* (New York: Doubleday,
    1906), 100.

58. Thomas Aquinas, *Summa Theologiae,* II-II, Q. 129, Art. 6, ad. 2, trans.
    T. C. O'Brien (London: Blackfriars, 1964), 119.

59. Douglass, *Life and Times of Frederick Douglass,* in *Autobiographies,*
    896.

Chapter 9: The Fragile Brilliance of Glass

1. Augustine, *City of God,* trans. Henry Bettenson (New York: Penguin,
   1984), 138 (IV.3).

2. Ibid.

3. Benjamin Franklin, quoted in James Madison, *Notes of Debates in the
   Federal Convention of 1787* (New York: W. W. Norton, 1987), 659.

4. Ibid., 653.

5. Ibid., 654.

6. Benjamin Franklin, *Autobiography,* in *Writings,* ed. J. A. Leo Lemay
   (NY: Library of America, 1987), 1390.

A MORAL TAXONOMY

H umility is the first of the virtues," Oliver Wendell Holmes
Jr. said, "for other people." When it comes to one's own life,
HUMILITY is among the hardest of virtues because of the
HONESTY it demands about one's own soul. Humility reveals to
man that he is not his own maker and that the individual is not
the measure of all things. Reminding us of our imperfect nature
and the human propensity to evil, humility calls us to overcome
our tendency to self-aggrandize. It asks that we put others first in
thought, word, and deed. Humility requires that we admit when
we wrong and then change course. It makes one unafraid to ask
forgiveness, and it demands that we use any power granted to us to
promote PEACE, do JUSTICE, and act with MERCY.

Among contemporary virtues, humility is often slighted as the
wimpy one—if seen as a virtue at all. In fact, humility is strong
because of the order it brings to a soul. As a check against the
UNHEALTHY PRIDE, or ARROGANCE, that is marked by an inordinate LOVE OF SELF, humility helps us recall our dependence
upon the divine and each other. This reminder does not mean
servility or weakness but rather the proper recognition of one's
abilities and merit. Humility makes one a servant, never a slave.

It is a complement, not a contradiction, to HEALTHY PRIDE. Both are essential to the achievement of SELF-GOVERNMENT, or the rule of the passions by right reason and a conscience formed with care. Humility helps guard against the soul's rebellion in pride run amok. As Abigail Adams wrote in 1780 to her husband John, "Pride, vanity, envy, ambition, and malice are the ungrateful foes that combat merit and integrity. Though for a while they may triumph to the injury of the just and good, the steady, unwearied perseverance of virtue and honor will finally prevail over them."

Humility is often accompanied in a well-ordered soul by modesty and meekness. Contrary to popular misconception, MODESTY is not the underestimation of one's worth. Rather, it restrains the drive to recognition. In resisting the natural impulse to claim credit and crave praise, modesty is the anti-VANITY. MEEKNESS is the denial of the power of oppression. A RESILIENT and RESOLUTE virtue, meekness prizes COMPASSION. Though people who are modest, meek, and humble are chastened by an awareness of their fallibility, this does not mean that they are plagued by SELF-PITY or low self-esteem. In fact, humility lets the theological virtue of hope shine most brightly. It is the striving of an arrogant man, when proven futile, that deteriorates into self-pity and ends in despair.

Humility builds one up. It commends PIETY without pomposity; it urges KINDNESS without regard to reward. Humility is a prerequisite to PRUDENCE, or practical wisdom; it permits one to make decisions less on who gets the glory and more on the merits of the matter at hand. Humility enables COURAGE and points WISDOM in the right direction. It is the backbone of TEMPERANCE and a helpmate to JUSTICE. Humility is the crown of the virtues. By enabling human beings to avoid the temptation of GLORY and FAME, humility makes possible lasting greatness of soul, or MAGNANIMITY. The exceedingly rare combination of humility and magnanimity in the lives of extraordinary individuals is the story of this book.

SUGGESTED FURTHER READING

Arnn, Larry P. *The Founders' Key: The Divine and Natural Connection Between the Declaration and the Constitution and What We Risk By Losing It* (Nashville, TN: Thomas Nelson, 2012).

Benestad, Brian J., ed. *Ernest Fortin: Collected Essays*, 3 vols. (Lanham, MD: Rowman and Littlefield, 1996).

Brookhiser, Richard. *James Madison* (New York: Basic Books, 2011).

Faulkner, Robert. *The Case for Greatness: Honorable Ambition and Its Critics* (New Haven, CT: Yale University Press, 2007).

Guelzo, Allen C. *Abraham Lincoln as a Man of Ideas* (Carbondale, IL: Southern Illinois University Press, 2009).

Hallowell, John H. *Main Currents in Modern Political Thought* (New York: Henry Holt and Company, 1950).

Hayward, Steven F. *Greatness: Reagan, Churchill and the Making of Extraordinary Leaders* (New York: Three Rivers Press, 2005).

Landy, Marc, and Sidney M. Milkis. *Presidential Greatness* (Lawrence, KS: University Press of Kansas, 2000).

Mahoney, Daniel J. *Aleksandr Solzhenitsyn: The Ascent from Ideology* (Lanham, MD: Rowman and Littlefield, 2001).

Manent, Pierre. *The City of Man*, trans. Marc A. LePain (Princeton, NJ: Princeton University Press, 1998).

Morrisey, Will. *Self-Government, The American Theme: Presidents of the Founding and the Civil War* (Lanham, MD: Lexington Books, 2005).

Myers, Peter C. *Frederick Douglass: Race and the Rebirth of American Liberalism* (Lawrence, KS: University Press of Kansas, 2008).

Schall, James V. *Reason, Revelation, and the Foundations of Political Philosophy* (Baton Rouge, LA: Louisiana State University Press, 1987).

Spalding, Matthew. *We Still Hold These Truths: Rediscovering Our Principles, Reclaiming Our Future* (Wilmington, DE: ISI Books, 2009).

ACKNOWLEDGMENTS

The humble strength exemplified in the thought of the late Ernest Fortin challenged all those around him to reflect more clearly on the place of politics in the eternal order. I am grateful to have been among his students at Boston College. Matthew Lamb's grand journey through Augustine's *City of God*, Robert Faulkner's presentation of high ambition, David Lowenthal's argument for Lincoln's magnanimity, Daniel Mahoney's keen attention to the ideological temptation in politics, and Pierre Manent's incisive treatment of the tension between humility and greatness of soul all helped to shape the argument in this book. Fellowships from the Earhart, Bradley, and Pew Foundations supported my early work on this project.

I landed at Boston College for my graduate studies in part because of the excellent guidance given to me by my undergraduate teachers Robert Eden, Mickey Craig, and the late Aleksandras Shtromas, all at Hillsdale College. Their love for the study of politics was contagious; their friendship has been a blessing.

Hillsdale College President Larry Arnn has taught me much about America's founding. I am grateful for having had the opportunity of working for him, and my alma mater, for now over a decade. My colleagues at Hillsdale's Kirby Center for Constitutional Studies and Citizenship are a pleasure to work with. I thank Margie King for her assistance in early work on the manuscript. My students in Washington make possible a rich exchange of ideas in a place where self-interestedness too often carries the day.

Many other friends and colleagues have informed the arguments in this book and encouraged me in the writing of it. Will Morrisey, Dennis Teti, John McFarland, David Joy, Tony Williams, and Joe Cella read the manuscript with care; it is much improved for their suggestions.

This book would not exist but for the confidence in it showed by my editor, Joel Miller. Thanks to him and the outstanding team at Thomas Nelson who have shepherded this project to completion.

Several months ago, about the time that my two boys sensed that I was about to disappear again with "the book," the older one, Walker, suggested to Michael, the younger, that we should have one last fire in the fireplace for the season. "Let's make it as big as daddy's head," he said. For their joyful and raucous impatience throughout the last two years I will forever be grateful.

My wife's patience is as wondrous as the rest of her soul. As my dearest friend and editor, she improved this book immeasurably. As my wife and soulmate, she gladdens everything. I dedicate this book to Anna, with all my love forever.

ABOUT THE AUTHOR

David J. Bobb is founding director of the Hillsdale College Kirby Center for Constitutional Studies and Citizenship, in Washington, D.C., and a lecturer in politics. Previously he was director of the college's Hoogland Center for Teacher Excellence, a national civic education program.

He earned a Ph.D. in political science at Boston College, where he received Earhart, Bradley, and Pew Foundation fellowships. Formerly he was a research associate at the Boston-based Pioneer Institute for Public Policy Research.

He has written articles and reviews for the *Wall Street Journal*, *Washington Times*, *Boston Herald*, *Claremont Review of Books*, *Perspectives on Political Science*, and the *American Spectator*, among other publications, and is a contributing editor to *The U.S. Constitution: A Reader*. He has spoken widely to audiences in twenty-five states on topics including education reform, civic engagement, the American Constitution, and religion and politics.

David and his wife Anna live with their two sons, Walker and Michael, in Washington, D.C.

HUMILITYBOOK.COM

INDEX